MOLIÈRE

Borgo Press Books by GEORGE SAND

Molière: A Play in Five Acts

MOLIÈRE

A PLAY IN FIVE ACTS

GEORGE SAND

Translated and Adapted by Frank J. Morlock

THE BORGO PRESS
MMXII

MOLIÈRE

Copyright © 2002, 2012 by Frank J. Morlock

FIRST BORGO PRESS EDITION

Published by Wildside Press LLC

www.wildsidebooks.com

DEDICATION

*Dedicated to my daughter, Michelle,
Just for being you*

CONTENTS

CAST OF CHARACTERS 9
ACT ONE 11
ACT TWO 51
ACT THREE 87
ACT FOUR 115
ACT FIVE 141
TRANSLATOR'S NOTE 181
ABOUT THE AUTHOR 183

CAST OF CHARACTERS

Molière

Cavalier

Brecourt

Duparc, called Big René

Baron

Louis XIV

A fine wit

A Marquis

Chief Mechanic

Brigadier

Madelaine Béjart

Armande Béjart

Pierrette LaForet, servant of Molière

Madelaine, daughter of Molière

Two pretty ladies

An old lady

Workers, ladies and gentlemen, musicians, etc.

ACT ONE

The Limousin. Trees and rocks on a height. A crossroads in the distance. Brecourt is in a horse-drawn cart which stops on the stage.

Brecourt (getting out of the cart)

This place seems to me disposed as we would like for a resting place, food, and a nap. Indeed, the peasants told us we would find a shaded fountain at the top of the slope.

(Duparc is coming down a path and lowering his musket. He whistles for his dogs.)

Duparc

Tiburce! Artaban!

Brecourt

Will you forget your mutts for a while and come help me to unpack our provisions? We will be fine here. The carriage cushions for the ladies' seats. The hamper with food. All nice! We won't lack anything. We are set. And suppose we were to light a fire?

(Duparc helps Brecourt unload a big, square hamper, some

cushions and diverse utensils from the cart.)

Duparc

Fire? What for?

Brecourt

To cook the game you proceeded to kill on the way.

Duparc

Bad joke. You only think of your gut, and forget this poor horse who's worth more than all of us.

(Duparc lets the horse out of its harness.)

Brecourt

I think first of those of my species.

Duparc

Our species is the worst of all, Brecourt. The men are worth nothing. Are our companions on the way?

Brecourt (looking to the rear of the theatre and leaning on the rocks)

Our chief is climbing the side and the ladies are coming on their light feet, beating the bushes like school kids on vacation.

Duparc

Yes, yes, according to their custom, always laughing, gossiping, or standing around gaping, while we die of hunger and thirst waiting for them! My stomach is hollow. All right, I'm going to put this poor horse in the shade. My dogs have already found a good corner. (leaving with the horse)

Brecourt (alone)

Who could believe that misanthrope is, on the boards, the best laugh getter in the troupe? The public never suspects the true feelings of the joyous Fat René. The public never knows that the mask which laughs and grimaces is often stuck to the face of the comedian by his tears!

(Pierrette, very poorly dressed with a torn and patched shirt, enters from the right.)

Pierrette (turning back and speaking to someone offstage)

Come, young ladies, be joyous and gay, and don't run through the wheat and ruin your beautiful clothes.

Brecourt (aside, observing Pierrette from the depths of the stage)

Who the devil is this pretty little peasant talking to? To her geese—God forgive me.

Pierrette (thinking herself alone)

Oh! That's what those young girls must be warned against often! Because you have such a light-weight brain. Not like me, always thinking of something. Let's see, what was I thinking about so carefully? I was really thinking about eating—but damn—I don't even have a crumb to nibble on. Could go to sleep—but I also have to think about watching my geese—and these two ideas never will work together. Damn. I really would be bored, being all alone on the mountain if I didn't have my sharp wit to keep me company. Still, they say at the farm that I am simple. (changing her voice and imitating someone) "A big goof who is sixteen and doesn't know a thing." (returning to her own voice) Oh, yeah, if someone showed me something, I'd know something. (noticing Brecourt) Oh, oh. (starts to move away)

Brecourt

Well, now, my child, did I frighten you so much?

Pierrette

Oh, eh, a whole lot, sir. Don't hurt me. I wasn't talking to you.

Brecourt

You're a real savage, my sweet—and yes—you were talking all by yourself just now—very freely.

Pierrette

You were listening to me, then? Look—who would have known it? But I didn't say anything bad about you. I wasn't thinking just about you.

Brecourt

I believe it. Anyway, I don't intend to hurt you. Here—you know what this is? (showing her a coin)

Pierrette

I don't know much. I don't know how to count money.

Brecourt

You don't earn anything from your life as a goose-girl?

Pierrette

Indeed, I do. I earn my bread. They give me shoes in the bargain.

Brecourt

Well, how'd you like to earn this money?

Pierrette

Certainly not, sir, if it requires me to do something against the King's good.

Brecourt

Ha! Ha! You stand for the King, do you?

Pierrette

Me? Damn—I don't know.

Brecourt

Do you know who the King is?

Pierrette

I've never seen him.

Brecourt

But, you fear rebels?

Pierrette

Oh, yes, for sure.

Brecourt

Who are these rebels?

Pierrette

Damn, they say that—my word, I don't know. You say so many things that I don't get. They talk like that at home: that you must act for the good of the King—and those—I don't know much more about it.

Brecourt

Never mind. I won't ask you any more about it. Would you like to assist us, my friends and me, in having lunch under those trees?

Pierrette

And, where are your friends?

Brecourt (escorting her to the rear)

Here—see them climbing up here?

Pierrette

Oh—the fashionable, pretty people, all in brave city clothes. We don't often see people like that around here. But, if they want to ask me to lunch—I have nothing to give them—first of all.

Brecourt (pointing to the basket and placing it in the middle of the stage)

We've got everything we need right here, and you'll have your share if you help us.

Pierrette

What have I got to do? Hold your horse? Oh, I know all about horses. I'll twist his reins so he cannot escape. But, who's that gentleman coming this way? Is he a priest? He's all dressed in black.

Brecourt

No, he's an actor. It's our boss.

Pierrette

Oh, he's an actor? I don't know what that is, but it's not my custom—

(Molière, on foot, leads in another horse pulling a cart. Brecourt goes and tries to help him.)

Brecourt

Well, Molière. Haven't I found a pretty dining spot? I've seen to everything, for I've already got a page. (pointing to Pierrette) There's a spring under the rocks where we can fill our canteens.

Molière

That's your job, my dear Brecourt, to be the first. See—ladies, isn't he a model man? In the theatre, on tour, everywhere, isn't it he who is always working for the pleasure of others?

Armande

He has to be nice for two. For his friend, Duparc, and for himself.

Molière

Duparc also comes at all your commands, Miss Armande.

Brecourt (to Pierrette who now holds the horse)

Let's go give them hay.

Pierrette

Oh, I really know how to care for the animals. Say, ladies, will you watch mine while I do that?

Armande

What do you mean?

Pierrette (pointing to the wings from which she entered)

Yes—my geese, who are over there in the tall wheat.

(Pierrette and Brecourt exit with the horse.)

Armande (laughing)

Good, count on it.

Molière

Well, gang, you see—you wanted to follow my wandering fortune, and often I can only offer you a seat of turf and a roof of leaves. It's much too wearying and adventurous for delicate women.

Madelaine

Up to now I haven't felt tired, and our adventures seem to me more diverting than intimidating. I love it, this vagabond life and I didn't imagine it to be as agreeable as it is in your company.

Molière (looking at Armande from time to time)

You say that not to hurt me, well knowing that I would like to give you all the comforts, and that I suffer from being powerless to take the barbs from your path. What a generous charity is yours, Madelaine. Only a word from you provides courage and consolation.

Madelaine

You don't seem to recognize yourself, Molière; for you are my model—and it's you I force myself to resemble to be satisfied with myself.

Armande

Oh, my God—what compliments! Are you both playing a role?

Madelaine

I speak my thoughts—which ought to be yours as well, Armande.

Armande

Oh, my thought—well here it is for the moment: I'm hot, I'm hungry, I'm bushed.

Molière

Poor little beauty. Let's hurry the lunch.

(Molière goes to the basket. Armande rises.)

Madelaine

Not before our friends who are taking the trouble to be here to begin with us. Don't indulge the child, my friend. Doesn't she have to learn to be patient and suffer like the others? She wanted to travel with us, she wanted to be an actress. I found her to be still too young, but you forced me to let her go—and now that she's here—she must learn to bear things without complaining.

Molière (to Armande, who hangs her head)

Your sister is, alas, right, Armande. You've got to be patient. (he places his hands behind him, raises the cover of the basket, picks out food and surreptitiously passes it to Armande) You must be temperate and believe what your sister tells you.

Armande

All right, I'll try. Thanks for the lesson, my good friend. I am going to take a walk while waiting for lunch, to exercise my patience. (leaves, nibbling)

Madelaine

Molière, Molière! You love that little girl too much!

Molière

I love her as if she were my child.

Madelaine

As if she were your child! You are not more than thirty—and she's soon to be fifteen. Are you of age to be a tutor?

Molière

It seems so, yes. I think that she is your niece, and that I am her father, because I consider you to be my sister. The solid friendship which unites me to you, Madeleine fills my life with courage and strength; the holy tenderness I have for Armande cheers up my leisure and softens my heart. It's from you that I receive whatever good I have in my soul—and it's to her that I wish to have the power to confer a benefit that is owed more to her than to me.

Madelaine

You don't love us in the same way, I know that—but doesn't she have the best part? It's eight years since you and I began sharing the same burdens and the same fortune—and it's hardly six months since my sister has been with us—and already she occupies you more than is right.

Molière

What! Madeleine, does friendship exist with jealousy?

Madelaine (shaking)

Friendship is jealous of confidence. Listen, Molière; I want yours, I demand it. Show me the bottom of your heart. Do you feel love for Armande? If that is so, I demand that you do not hide it away any more from me. I will redouble my efforts to render my sister worthy of you, and I will serve her faithfully as a tutor and mother—to join her fate to yours as soon as she's of age to marry.

Molière (a bit moved)

Are you speaking seriously, Madeleine?

Madelaine (moved, but containing herself)

I swear it to you, by our friendship.

Molière

Well, I, by reason of the respect I have for you, I swear that I've never thought of marriage without fear and aversion. I'm the man on earth least capable of fixing himself in eternal chains. Not that I have a flighty character—inconstancy is ingratitude, and anyway—I'd be too jealous to give my wife the example of infidelity, but to have a companion, you have to make her happy, and mine would never find anything of interest in the things that preoccupy me—you know, quite well—I have only one passion—that's theatre—that I've sacrificed everything to it—my relatives, my future, myself. Heir to certain commercial funds, and of a situation lucrative enough in the King's household, son of a legal family, a graduate if you please! Haven't you seen me leave it all to attach myself to a wretched profession, that the world considers degrading? I was thrust by an unknown force—by a stubbornness of my destiny even stronger than my will. And still, though I don't see the end of my disappointments, of my troubles, and my obscurity—nothing will make me relinquish my plan. I intend to give all my time,—all my attention, all my thoughts. I will not allow myself to be distracted, neither by feelings of my heart, nor by burdens of the family. You see clearly then, I ought not to marry—at least until I become very rich, very celebrated—(smiling) Which is not very likely. What do you think?

Madelaine

I know your determination, and I am concerned with your interests to the extent that neither of us should marry. However, on that score, Molière, you ought not to love my sister, and I have reason to be uneasy.

Molière

No, Madeleine, you have no reason to be—for I'm a gallant man and you know so, quite well.

Madelaine

Then, you will give me your honest and considered word that you will always look on Armande with the eyes of a brother?

Molière

Yes, my young friend, receive it before God.

Madelaine

I believe it, and I count on it.

Brecourt (from the rear of the stage)

Molière! Hey! Molière!

(Molière goes towards Brecourt.)

Madelaine (aside)

I believe it, and I count on it—and yet I'm worried.

Brecourt

Here's a nice piece of luck! We have everything for lunch except some bread—which we forgot. (pointing to Pierrette) But, this little girl says there's a farm near here where we can get some. I'm off.

Molière

No, it's up to me to do something for the others. Stay put.

Pierrette

Oh, it's quite close. Look—at the end of this field.

Madelaine (to Molière)

I am going with you.

Molière

Fine, come. But, where's Armande?

Brecourt (looking toward the wings)

There—on the very road you are going to take. As for me, I am going to fetch water. (to Pierrette) You, watch our stuff.

(All exit except Pierrette.)

Pierrette

Oh, golly! There's no danger. Not many people go that road. It's all the same. They tell me to watch. I am going to watch. (sitting against a tree, with her back to the basket, she begins to yawn) This way I can watch my geese—who are there—very nice—

they're all sleeping. Oh, lazy ones, to sleep like that at midday. (she falls asleep)

Cavalier (in the crossroads, striking his horse who is resting)

Come on! Courage, cursed beast. Are you already winded? (now whipping the horse who runs away) Eat, go to sleep, croak, do what you want and go to the devil. (coming forward, wiping his brow) I'm as tired as my mount and if I thought about it, I'd let myself fall. But the will must serve man, especially during great dangers. Ho! This place seems to be occupied. (examining the cart and reading the inscription: "Props of Molière") Molière—Now, what is that? (puts his head into the cart and comes out with several theatrical accessories) Armor, rapiers, pikes of golden wood. These are not men of war—but country actors. I ought to get a bargain. They'll have to give me their horse. Where are they, then? (seeing Pierrette) Hey, shortie! (shaking her) Hey, up and at 'em. Wake up! Answer!

Pierrette

Oh, what's going on? Are you one of the people who are going to lunch here?

Cavalier

I wish. Hot damn! Yes, I am. What are you going to eat?

Pierrette

Here, this basket of food. Only the bread is missing, and they've gone to find it.

Cavalier

Bread! Oh! No big deal! (sitting on the basket and raising its cover)

Pierrette

Are you going to start to eat without waiting for your friends? That's not very nice.

Cavalier

Is that so?

Pierrette (aside)

Oh, what evil eyes he has! Maybe he's a thief. I'm going to warn the others, I am. (she escapes)

Cavalier

Nice meeting, God's my witness. Fortune follows me everywhere. Come on—with confidence and audacity, and the goose hangs high. (beginning to carve a fowl) My seven men ought to have returned. Seven men against all France, yes—but I am the eighth.

(Brecourt, holding a stick behind him, approaches without the Cavalier observing him. After watching the Cavalier for a moment, Brecourt straddles the basket facing the Cavalier.)

Brecourt

Enjoy your dinner—my friend.

Cavalier (taking a bottle from the basket)

Many thanks—to your health.

(Brecourt raises his stick, but the Cavalier rapidly pulls a pistol from his belt.)

Cavalier

Easy, my friend. I'm hungry. I'm thirsty. I'm in a hurry. But, I have money and I'll pay those who oblige me—and kill anyone who bothers me.

Brecourt (drawing his rapier)

Kill—if you can, for I am very determined to bother you.

Cavalier (putting aside his pistol and drawing his rapier)

If you take those tones—fine. (aside) In my opinion, I am doing this gentleman ill. A fight can only slow me down.

Brecourt

Well, sir, I am at your service. Do you recoil already?

Cavalier

Not at all; but shall we cut each other's throats for so little? Sell me your share of this dinner, for if I had a kingdom, I would give it right now for a slice of bread.

Brecourt

Sir, I am not a grocer, and do not keep an inn. I'm much distressed to shame you, but, it's necessary, if you please, that you receive a little lesson for having touched things confided to my care without permission. Choose either rapiers or sticks.

Cavalier

So—you insist. I am sorry for you, I swear.

(They cross swords.)

Molière (entering with the others and separating their swords with his cane)

Stop it, gentlemen! Brecourt, what's all this?

Brecourt

Leave me alone, leave me alone, Molière. I'm by way of teaching a tourist with too much appetite a little lesson. I surprised him plundering our provisions.

Molière

This case is grave because we too have a great appetite. Look here, famished sir, what have you to say in your defense?

Cavalier

Sir, since you don't appear to me disposed to see this in a tragic light, I will confess to you. I acted a little cavalierly. The fatigue to which I am succumbing can alone excuse me. I intended to leave my purse in payment of my pillage. I offered it to your comrade, who refuses to listen. He's a bit of a hot head.

Molière (going close to the cavalier and examining him)

He's the sweetest and the best of men, but proud and very brave—and there's nothing in his character which should surprise you, for you yourself—

Cavalier

Well, what is it? Why are you looking at me that way?

Molière

Because, may I die, but I know you.

Cavalier (lowering his voice, but in a commanding tone)

You are mistaken! You don't know me at all.

Molière (low)

That commanding tone. That Eagle's look. Oh, pardon me, sir, I know you very well, and whoever sees you once, will not forget you. (aloud) Brecourt, I know this gentleman. He's a gallant man, though a little abrupt. I have spoken to him. Serve him lunch, set out one more place.

(The other characters busy themselves, coming and going from the rear of the theatre.)

Cavalier

You say you know me? Well—lying is distasteful to me, and even to save my destiny, I wouldn't lower myself to it. Look—what are you planning to do? (turning and looking behind him) You are three against me, but you ought to know, even were there ten of you, you won't take me easily.

Molière

Were we as many as twenty, I know. Have a good enough opinion of me to think that I yield from respect more than from fear, believe also, sir, that it is not your rank which dazzles me, but to genius, to valor, to misfortune, perhaps, that I feel compelled to pay respect.

Cavalier

To misfortune? Yes or no—who can say? God is the Master. You, sir, you appear to me to be a man of sense. Keep my secret, and count on it, if I live, you will be greatly rewarded one day.

Molière

Sir, although the King has not given me the duty of protecting his kingdom, I could seize your person by violence—(the cavalier smiles)

—or by treachery. (the cavalier shivers) So, for violence, I cannot help having respect for your person—and as for treachery—sir, look at me, and see if you think I am capable of it.

Cavalier (after a pause, during which he looks at Molière)

Man never saw a more masculine and more honest face! I trust you.

Molière

You do well to do so. (to his friends) Come friends, to table—to table. (to Cavalier) This is a sort of metaphor. Each does here what he can—and you know better than we what it is to live in the country.

Brecourt (to Cavalier)

The gentleman has won his case! Well, since you are a friend of Molière, take it. I regret having hindered you.

(They sit down, the ladies on their cushions, the men on some stumps or some rocks which they place around the basket which they use as a table.)

Molière

This gentleman is a man of quality. I don't have the honor of being his friend, but I've had the honor of seeing him at court where I was through inheriting offices attached to the person of His Majesty Louis XIII.

Cavalier (shaking)

The late King.

Molière

I followed the King and I saw Richelieu, on his deathbed, give to the executioner the heads of Cinq-Mars and de Thou. He was cruel, but he was great, like tragedy. What we see today is only comedy.

Cavalier

Ah! You think so?

Brecourt

We share the world's opinion.

Duparc

It's not even good comedy, 'cause it's ridiculous, but not entertaining.

Cavalier

And Mazarin is not, in your opinion, a Richelieu?

Duparc

I don't know about your opinion. I'm not used to hiding mine. Mazarin—

Brecourt

Mazarin is whatever you please. Right now I am for him as Turenne is for him.

Cavalier

Ah—you are for Turenne?

Brecourt

Gad, yes, sir—for I served under his orders—and no one can tell me he is not the greatest man of these times.

Molière (seeing the Cavalier's agitation)

The gentleman thinks so himself, for he is attached to his service.

Cavalier (starting)

Me?

Molière

Why, yes. Didn't you tell me you were entrusted with an important mission and that you are busy with it?

Cavalier (smiling)

Yes, yes. You are right. That's the way it is, which must serve as my excuse to this gentleman, (pointing to Brecourt) for having violently laid hands on his preparations for this country meal. (to Brecourt) Since you wear the armor of war, my brave fellow, you know quite well that hunger and thirst are two big devils that don't waste time talking.

Brecourt

Well, yes, I admit that; they often act as you do—treating their own country as a conquered province. So much the worse for the poor peasant! So much the worse for the poor traveler.

Duparc

Still, he became an actor from disgust at his job of pillager—and for the sole purpose of becoming a good citizen again.

Molière (laughing)

The gentleman will determine later, if to expiate his sins, he agrees to play your role.

Brecourt

While waiting, I give him the health of the Great Turenne.

Cavalier

I'll drink to that, and that of the King, if it seems good to you.

Madelaine

I, woman that I am, propose a toast to the Queen. She is as

unfortunate as he is.

Armande

As for me, I drink to the Prince! I am young. Long live the Prince!

Cavalier

Truly, my beautiful child?

Armande

I have a contradictory disposition and cannot bear to march like others.

Molière (laughing)

Armande is just to herself.

Armande

And you, Duparc, called Big René, aren't you drinking to anyone? Well, I want you to do me justice, and I propose a toast to the health of your two dogs, Tiburce and Artaban.

Duparc (raising his glass)

Long live the dogs! They alone are honest and faithful in this world.

Pierrette (seated on the ground near Armande)

Oh, well—hail to the geese. They are good creatures, too. They don't have a drop of malice.

Molière

Toast the beasts as much as you wish. The most humble creatures are the work of the Great Artificer of the Universe, whose beautiful nature is a temple open to all men, even a poor excommunicated actor. But since we are by way of making toasts, let's drink to the poor people of France who pay for the music at all the feasts and the trumpets at every war! What do you say to that, dear guest?

Cavalier

Long live France and it's people. So be it!

Molière

Alas, France—where is it at this point in time?

Cavalier

Sir, it is where it's true interests are—and not everyone can be judge of that.

Molière

There are quite a few theories about that, but I am a poor man who is not very practical and who goes moralizing and philosophizing in my way over evident facts. I think, hopefully I do not offend you, that today no party represents France. The Old Regime, the Young Regime, the parliament, the people of the towns and the country who fight, sometimes for this one, sometimes for that one, without knowing which way to turn—all these scarves, all these flags, only represent passions, interests, ambitions—of the mighty; and of the poor—ignorance, restlessness, despair. In the midst of your conflicts, France is dying—the countryside laid to waste, religion is corrupted and the arts perish. Well, here's a being innocent of any passions. A child of fifteen who calls himself Louis the XIV and who, by the will of God is invited to personify the unity of France. He alone can reign without calling foreigners into France, and thereby proves his cause is, during the times in which we live, legitimate. Good God—what an education the fractious are providing this poor child,-- an education in civil war—which reminds me—but I am boring you with a tale which is inopportune.

Cavalier

Concerning the young King? Speak, speak. That will interest everyone.

Molière

Well, it was a day that the King, still in diapers, wept a great deal, and could not be comforted. Her Majesty, the Queen thought of sending for Scaramouche.

Cavalier

Scaramouche?

Molière

Yes, Tiberio Fiorelli, the famous Scaramouche, a very pleasant actor, who, like all the professional clowns had a very melancholy disposition. I was his student, and he took me with him to carry his guitar—his dog, his cat, his monkey—and his parakeet. The King didn't stop crying—he made his animals jump and dance, but the King wept even more. Then Scaramouche requested they put the King in his arms and they did. Suddenly, stopping all his grimaces and looking at the royal child with a very severe air, he said: "Oh King, keep your tears for the day when you learn to know mankind." This was spoken in such a very grave tone, and with eyes so full of pity, and struck the child like a prophesy, you would have thought he understood, for his tears stopped abruptly. With his little hands, he caressed the cheeks and the long moustache of Scaramouche. The Queen gave him a beautiful gold chain, saying: "So, Scaramouche, you are much wiser than we think, or you speak more truly than you know."

Cavalier

Your story is pleasant, but what moral do you draw from it?

Molière

That the time has come for the King to weep, indeed, if he loves France, and to scream very loud if he wants to save her.

Cavalier

Let him shout then: "Help me, my friends" and his true friends will save him.

Molière

His true friends are not those who are trying to dethrone him, or to shred the remnants of the nation.

Cavalier

In fact, sir—

Pierrette (who left a few moments before, returns all breathless)

Hey, sir, hey—your horse, that you left with his bridle on, is jumping around like the devil himself and trying to eat the others.

Cavalier

Ah—so much the better. I thought he was done for. (going out)

Armande (to Molière)

Who is that guy? He doesn't seem to think like you at all.

Molière

I will tell you soon, when he's gone. Pack up, everybody.

(Brecourt and Duparc begin to pack up the utensils.)

Pierrette

Oh! You're going so soon? Just as I was getting used to you, and I'm going to be bored not to have anyone to speak to.

Molière

Eh! This kid is sweet. She doesn't look stupid.

Pierrette

Oh, indeed, sir, I am stupid. They tell me so, all the time, and no one wants to keep company with me. But, I'm in good spirits anyhow! And, if you could take me to fatten your fowl, to watch your geese or milk your cows—

Molière

I'd really like to, but the trouble is, I haven't any such creatures. Look, do you know how to help and care for people?

Pierrette

Try me! I can learn.

Molière

Ladies, you don't have a maid, and you're looking for one. Won't this one please you with her good humor?

Madelaine

Indeed. What's your name, child?

Pierrette

Pierrette LaForet, at your service, Miss.

Madelaine

Don't you have relatives who would be opposed to it?

Pierrette

I have neither father, nor mother, nor uncles, nor aunts. I am a child of God. I was found in the middle of the woods, and that's why they gave me the name of LaForet.

Molière

She's got wit without being aware of it. Take her, ladies. What do you earn?

Pierrette

My keep, which I really need. It's a pound of bread for each day of the year.

Madelaine

That goes without saying. And your wages?

Pierrette

Oh, I don't understand anything about such things. You will give me whatever you please.

Molière

Well, your candor proves you've got a good heart. Come with us, and you won't be sorry.

Pierrette

Oh, you bet—right away! I'm going to return my geese and thank the people of the farm. (leaves)

Molière

Friends, leave me alone for a bit with our guest—for here he is, ready to leave.

(All exit except Molière and the Cavalier.)

Cavalier

Before being on my way, Mr. Molière, I want to thank you for your hospitality, and to offer you my services. I think your character doesn't agree with your profession. Wouldn't you like to change it?

Molière

No, Prince, I love it, this situation. I want to live in it and to die in it.

Cavalier

Well, you are, I suppose, a serious tragic actor. These troubled times will pass. Then you could be engaged at the Hotel Bourgogne.

Molière

My ambition is not so great.

Cavalier

Or you have a greater? Speak.

Molière

May the Prince pardon me, but I love only the verse of the great Corneille, and I feel myself unequal to it.

Cavalier

Modesty.

Molière

Not at all. My mood is jovial, and not heroic.

Cavalier

You prefer comedy?

Molière

Yes, but I am only amused by those I create myself.

Cavalier

Ah! You're an author?

Molière

Not at all. I only write sketches on which my comrades and I embroider the impromptu dialogues after the manner of the Italians.

Cavalier

That type requires great wit.

Molière

It needs much of nature and observation of human characters. The exercise pleases and interests me more than any book.

Cavalier

Well, this entertainment is pleasing to educated people, as well as the people, and if I enter into my estate—

Molière

Don't promise me anything, Milord, for to content me, you would have to engage my entire troupe—of whom you've only seen a few here. All the members are not good—yet I will never abandon them to the world for anything. These poor folks depend on me to resist the rigor of fate. For now we have only a boon to ask of you.

Cavalier

Speak quickly, for I'm in a hurry to grant it.

Molière (smiling)

And to leave. Well, Prince, it would be to submit to the King. To end this civil war which disturbs us and wrongs us deeply—and tosses us from province to province—through many mishaps and perils. If you would grant us that, I would hold you quit of all the rest.

Cavalier (smiling)

We'll do our best, Mr. Molière. Pray for the King to help us a little. While waiting, please accept this little present in memory of the kind reception you gave me. (giving Molière a ring)

Molière

Sir, I did nothing to deserve this—Prince.

Cavalier (haughtily)

What! Sir—you pretend to have given me alms?

Molière

I know, these days, it is forbidden for a man in modest condition to refuse money from a great man, and refusal passes for impertinence, which places him in disgrace. But, we are not in an ordinary situation, and I speak the truth to you, as becomes an honest man, and it becomes a great man to listen. Prince, you are deliberately betraying the King and France. My duty would be to disrupt your plans at the risk of my life—and if I do not do so—it's because you are a hero and that, I hope, when this intoxication of vengeance you are now suffering from dissipates—you will yourself realize it. That's why I do not repent of showing you respect and having humbly shared my bread with you. But, it would be felony to my Sovereign to accept the least reward—and you must not insist further. If you blush, Milord, at receiving assistance from a poor devil of my type—forget it quickly. It's not to be thought that I will ever find myself in your way to make you recall it. (bows deeply and withdraws)

Cavalier (alone)

That fellow is very odd! He love and respects my person, which is sacred to him; he detests my work, which seems criminal to him! He's a man of great sense, whose bearing and words are singular. It's true his lovely profession places him outside the great interests and grand passions of this world. In what strange places is honesty found. (dreaming for a moment, then waking abruptly from his reverie) But, I haven't put myself en route with so much mystery and in the face of so many perils to let myself be stopped by such reasons.

(The Cavalier starts to leave and encounters Pierrette, who is returning.)

Cavalier

Hey! Little girl, I beg your pardon.

Pierrette

What's wrong now?

Cavalier

Come, my child. Your face reveals you are an honest person. You will take this ring for me and give it to the beautiful Armande—the youngest of the actresses, and you will beg her for me, to keep it as a souvenir of me. And this is for you, my girl. (giving her a ring and money, he leaves)

Pierrette

What do you give me money for? (raising her head) Right! Far away already. (looking at the rings) He's mounted on his horse. Didn't take long. He's off like a bolt of lightning. Oh, golly, he isn't dull, that fellow.

(Molière, Armande and the others return.)

Pierrette (to Armande)

Here, Miss! Here's a bauble which the gentleman who was here just now gave me for you. He said to tell you: "You will tell her—" Oh, blast—I can't remember what he told me to tell you.

Armande (taking the ring)

A present for me? Oh, beautiful ring. Look here, sis, a big diamond.

Madelaine

A present? And by what right does this stranger give you a present?

Armande

You're not going to take it away from me?

Madelaine

Yes, to give it to some poor person. You mustn't receive presents.

Armande (weeping)

See, Molière. She's a tyrant! My sister takes everything from me, and tricks me in everything.

Molière (to Madelaine)

Friend, you can leave this toy to the child. There's nothing to fear from the man who sent it to her. He's too far from us for him to have any design on her.

Armande

Is he a great person, then?

Molière

More than that—he's a great man.

Duparc

Really? I thought he had the look of a lunatic.

Brecourt

And to me, like a devil. I am not a coward and I think I've given proof of it. Well, while I crossed swords with him, his eyes penetrated me with flashes which prevented me from seeing his blade.

Molière

Brecourt, perhaps it would have been better if you had killed him, who knows? But, God's plans are hidden, and I felt a superior force which obliged me to preserve him from your blade.

Armande

My God—who is he, then? Oh, my dear Molière—tell me quick!

Molière (looking all around)

Has he gone?

Pierrette

Oh, he's far away!

Molière

Well, ladies, well, my friends, that man—was the Prince.

Madelaine

The Prince Condé?

Molière

The Great Condé.

Brecourt

Alone in the country when everyone thinks he's at the frontier?

Duparc

Damn! I understand. He's going to rejoin the Army of the Princes. He's going to march on Paris with the foreigners, kidnap the King and, perhaps, proclaim himself in the King's place—after having killed, or had killed, thousands of people who are worth more than he is. (rushing to the back of the stage and looking in the distance)

Brecourt

There he is, in the depth of the ravine. (Duparc shoulders his musket to shoot) He's going to fight Turenne. Shoot, Duparc.

Molière (lowering the weapon with his cane)

No, Duparc! That man, who has done so much good, may yet save France—if he realizes the wrong he has done. Turenne, the Great Turenne, yesterday, was with Condé against our King—tomorrow, perhaps, the King will be with Condé against Turenne. We live in times when the wisest commit great follies, when the craziest do unexpectedly great deeds. May God breathe on the spirit of vengeance. Sometimes misfortune is good. The little people learn that the quarrels of the great are not their quarrels. Well, ladies, isn't it time to be on our way? What's wrong, Armande? You are pale, and now you blush! What is agitating you so?

Armande (absorbed)

The Great Condé gave me a ring—to me! Oh, he'll never forget me. Alone, here, I drank his health! This beautiful ring! Now, sis, I defy you to take it away from me. I intend to wear it all my life. It's gorgeous, a diamond. It shines like the sun—like glory. To look at this, and to think of that man—it's dizzying.

Molière

Child, glory is turning your head!

Armande

Yes, yes, philosophize over it. You, who haven't got it, and will never get it. As for me, I want it, and I've got it—since the Great Condé paid attention to me!

Molière

There's more than one way to arrive at glory, Armande. But, you're no longer listening to me. (to Madelaine) She's lost her head, your kid sister, and you will see—from now on, she will scorn you. (lowering his voice) Well, do you still think I can plan to marry this proud one? (going to the carriage which gets ready to move off)

Madelaine (aside) God be blessed for this. Molière will never have her now.

CURTAIN

ACT TWO

At the Palace of Versailles. A waiting room, serving as a foyer for the actors. Mirrors, dressing tables. Doors in the back. A window giving on the gardens. A side door which leads to Molière's dressing room.

Molière, dressed as Sganarelle, comes out of his dressing room with Pierrette LaForet, who continues to dress him as he walks about.

Molière

Come on, come on, LaForet, that's enough. I'm ready—right?

(Molière looks at the grandfather clock near the chimney.)

Pierrette

Hey, Mr. Molière, give yourself time. What a hurry you are in.

Molière

I am not in a hurry. I am rushed. Look at the time.

Pierrette

There's no use rushing. The court will not rush for you. The court is still dining, and you have a long time to wait.

Molière

Never mind, my child. The King ordered the performance for six o'clock. Therefore, at six o'clock, it must be ready, and I, above all. It's for us to await the pleasure of the King, not the other way around.

Pierrette

Oh, very well, sir. But the King will wait for you a little. He waited for Lully this morning.

Molière

Really?

Pierrette

Oh, you didn't know that? Everyone in the house is talking about it.

Molière

But, Versailles is huge, and I can't be everywhere. What happened?

Pierrette

Well, sir, the King was waiting for—the—the—

Molière

The symphony?

Pierrette

That's it! Mr. Lully didn't find the music or the musicians to his plan. He made them rehearse two or three times. He was furious. He broke the violin. The King and the court were impatient. The King sent a page. Mr. Lully paid no attention. The King again sent a page. Nothing doing. The King sent a third page, who spoke like this: "For God's sake, Mr. Lully, the King is waiting for you." Upon which, Mr. Lully replied "The King is the master, right?" "Yes, sir." "In that case, sir, he is the waiting master."

Molière

That devil of a man. What a wit! Do you know if the King was angry?

Pierrette

They said he laughed heartily. So you see quite well, you don't need to worry yourself so. These gentlemen and ladies don't move as fast as you do. Miss Madelaine, I except—she is like you—always rushed, but the other one—oh! How lazy she is.

Molière

Armande?

Pierrette

It takes her an hour to adjust a ribbon or curl, and when she's finished, she looks at herself in her mirror with great satisfaction-even when everybody is calling for her.

Molière

You are unfair! For a long time now, she's been very hard working.

Pierrette

Yes, when you are watching her, 'cause she wants to please you.

Molière (shaking)

She wants to please me? What are you talking about?

Pierrette

She's clever! She's noticed that you are getting richer every day. Better treated by the great lords, better loved by the King—more famous at court than in the city—and she knows quite well it's going to be in her interest to satisfy you, to remain in your troupe, and to play the best parts. It wasn't like that when you were a little boss of a traveling barnstorming company that played in the fields as often as in the château! She defied you, she lashed out at you—she treated you rudely, and God knows, that you were not at that time, poor dear man! And now that you've gotten on a little, she flatters you, she manipulates you tactfully.

Molière

You are saying I've become rude?

Pierrette

I'm not angry with you about it. You had so much trouble! Now you seem tired.

Molière

I seem tired? Give me my make-up so I can fix my face.

Pierrette

Eh! Not yet! Your make-up will fall off before you go on stage. Look, take it easy for a bit. Sit in this armchair. Rest your legs. Do you know that for the two weeks we've been here you haven't had three hours sleep a night?

Molière

What of it? Do you take me for an old man? Because you are twenty-five, like Armande?

Pierrette

You are not old! But, you are fortyish and you are no longer young.

Molière

I hope that's true.

Pierrette

Not at all.

Molière

Yes, I tell you. Hold your plaguey tongue.

Pierrette

Ah, now you're becoming rude.

Molière (laughing)

No, I'm practicing a scene from the comedy I'm soon to play.

Pierrette

Why, it's true. It's from The Forced Marriage, where Sganarelle doesn't want to have the age that his friend falsely claims he has. But, you are not so old as Sganarelle, and you are not so mad as he to think of womanizing.

Molière

Why shouldn't I think about it?

Pierrette

Because you've always been against it.

Molière

That's not a good reason.

Pierrette

Oh, indeed, if you are interested, I know a woman for you: Miss Béjart.

Molière

Armande, are you crazy?

Pierrette

Oh, how your mind has changed! She is much too young and too much in love with herself. But, the elder Miss Béjart—who is a bit more mature, and still a pretty woman. She is a person, you see, who has heart, courage, and wit—almost as much as you.

Molière

Poor Madelaine!

Pierrette

Well, sir, don't you love her any more?

Molière

Indeed, with all my heart, as much as I esteem her. But, I've never had more for her than an honest friendship.

Pierrette

Well, Mr. Molière, in that case, what kind of friendship do you want to have from your wife?

Molière

You are right, Pierrette. (aside) This girl has terribly wise thoughts. (aloud) But, why the devil are you talking to me? I never intend to get married.

Pierrette

Oh, marry whoever you like! As for me, I will keep my place and serve your wife, were she the devil in petticoats.

(Brecourt and Duparc enter.)

Molière

Ah, my friends, you ready already? Good! Brecourt dressed as Pancrace; Duparc as Marphorius. You are very fine doctors, and will act well.

Brecourt

Don't worry: we know our roles, and the play pleases us. It's short, but it is gay, and the characters are as well drawn as they would be in a long play.

Duparc

Eh! In my opinion, that's the trouble. You start getting interested in the characters at the moment the play ends.

Molière

What do you want, my friend? Write a play, distribute the parts, stage it, rehearse it, and play it, all in forty-eight hours! With a ballet, yet!

Duparc

Yes, the play is only our excuse for the ballet, and the ballet an excuse for the King's desire to dance in it.

Pierrette

Oh, the King is not at all reasonable. To ask for four new plays in two weeks.

Molière

The King knew that Tartuffe was ready. As for the Princess

d'Élide, he allowed me to have help.

Duparc

If you think to do good work that way, so be it. That's your look out.

Brecourt

The least line of Molière is a master stroke and Tartuffe is ready to prove that the author of The Misanthrope hasn't lost anything.

Duparc (to Molière)

And have you read it—Tartuffe—to the King?

Molière

Yes.

Duparc

Completely?

Molière

Sure.

Duparc

And, he likes it?

Molière

The King is more indulgent than you, my friend. He told me he doesn't know which to prefer—The Misanthrope or Tartuffe.

Duparc

How marvelous for the King to say that.

Brecourt

Well, what about you?

Duparc

I don't like the subject of Tartuffe—it will make enemies for Molière.

Molière

Yes, at the court, but if the King and people are for me?

Duparc

Oh, you don't reckon with the nobility. You think they're dead because your young King mocks them and you ridicule them?

Brecourt

The Fronde is buried, thank God!

Molière

And, thanks to God, my friends, it's buried forever. The King is young, the King is handsome, and the King amuses himself. He runs at the ring and dances the ballet, and meanwhile, the King, who is, at bottom, grave, solid, attentive, and cold—governs and pursues his policy.

Duparc

No one would suspect it here! In the midst of tournaments, feasts, fireworks, and Chinese lanterns, the King puts on the face of grandly and lovingly courting his courtiers.

Molière

The King, seeming to ruin himself, ruins his nobility, who he attracts to his feasts. He intoxicates them with his seductions, he wipes them out with his magnificence, he abases the pride of the Châteaux and makes these proud lords gambol at his feet in the costumes of buffoons, they, who think themselves his equals in their provinces and who are learning from now on to efface themselves like little stars in the rays of the Versailles Sun.

Brecourt

You see precisely, Molière. The splendor of the King effaces that of the lords and, perhaps, prepares that of the lowly. The young nobility laughs at his feasts, because youth will amuse itself, even though it kills them. But, the old Frondeurs are not taken in, and twist their grey mustaches, accusing the King in whispers of only protecting villains.

Duparc

I grant you that, for the thing is plain enough, but, beware that the King has not also got bigots as well as go-getters. The posturing courtiers had to swallow the pill in The Misanthrope, but too many recognize themselves in Tartuffe, and they will ruin Molière in the books of the King, while waiting to ruin the King in the books of the people.

Brecourt

You always see things in black.

Duparc

I see them as they are.

Molière

May God protect us, my friends. And let's fulfill our task. A wise King, a strong man, encourages us to tell the truth. Let's say it—even if we must pay dearly for it, and he will disavow us for it one day.

(Armande and Madelaine enter, dressed in fantasy costumes.)

Madelaine

Well, gentleman, don't you hear the fanfare and the oboes? The King has left table and you've only got time to get on stage.

Molière (to Pierrette)

Eh—quick, Laforet. The white, the red, my eyebrows, my grey beard! You see plainly, I should have been ready. (arranging himself before the chimney mirror)

Brecourt

No reason to rush yet. The court will take more than a quarter of an hour to cross the enchanted grotto to the Château and be seated for the comedy.

Molière

You are all ready for the ballet, ladies? You look ready for an inspection.

Madelaine

I am ready.

Molière

And you, Armande?

Armande

I will be.

Duparc

Consider that the play begins in twenty minutes—that's less time than it ordinarily takes you to place a pin. The King won't give himself five minutes between the two raisings of the curtains to change into an Egyptian.

Molière

Where is Baron? Little Baron is also in the ballet.

Duparc

Oh, him! You cannot keep him. He'll have forgotten himself before some sheet of water, not to contemplate the tritons and the bronze naiads, but to satisfy the love of his own face like the handsome Narcissus of foolish memory.

Molière

What do you expect? He's handsome, that child, everybody likes him. Necessarily, he's a bit pleased with himself.

Duparc

Yes, yes, you do well to encourage him in that. It's your business to know what the finery of your adopted son costs you.

Brecourt

Well, if young Baron costs Molière some silk and some lace, it isn't any longer necessary to make a scene about these childish amusements!

Duparc

The plague of a child of that type whose downy hair begins to dance around the chin. Ask the chambermaids of the maids of honor who they are discovering now!

Brecourt

Does he cost your wife something?

Duparc

I don't care about my wife. Since she gallops like a page in the King's tournaments, it no longer seems that she's my wife, but rather say, my groom.

(Molière, having finished his make-up, makes all his actors go, and, on the point of leaving himself, he turns back towards Armande, who has remained near the window.)

Molière

You're staying, Armande? The success of my comedy doesn't interest you?

Armande

Indeed, I am following you. But I want to watch all the royal court pass by from here.

Molière

Ah, yes, all the handsome lords, all those marquises. (to Pierrette, with a kind of uneasiness) Stay with her, I have no need of you.

Pierrette

But, I want to see you act—and hold your cape in the wings. (Molière leaves, she follows him, saying in an aside) Miss Armande knows quite well how to take care of herself when she's all alone.

Armande (alone at the open window)

Ah, here's the King's troupe. The Count d'Armagnac, the Duke Saint-Aignan, the Marquis de Soiecourt, the most adroit at rings after His Majesty. The Marquis de Villeroy. (leaving the window) Molière cannot stand those Marquises—doubtless because he cannot be one. (arranging her face before the mirror) The nobility, needless to say, have nothing to acquire. That's why well-born people pardon commoners for having wit, while those never pardon them for being forced to bear it. This poor Molière. How jealous he is of me. In truth, I love it, and I feel great pleasure in enraging him. He's so nasty when he's in a rage and so good when he's finished scolding—and so dumb when he begs my pardon for the pain I've caused him.

(Armande goes back to the mirror, and doesn't turn when Baron enters stealthily.)

Baron (moved)

Ah, here you are alone, Miss Béjart?

Armande

That you, Baron? What do you want with me?

Baron

To see you for a moment, since I've found such a good opportunity.

Armande, Well, and so?

Baron

Eh, if that's your way of receiving me, I'll never dare to say anything to you.

Armande

It seems to me, you've got nothing to say to me that you haven't already written. (she turns toward him, pulling a letter from her pocket)

Baron

Oh, you got my letter! You read it! You've kept it, Armande.

(Baron starts to throw himself on his knees. Armande turns her back on him, and goes back to the mirror.)

Armande

Yes, I kept it, to show to Molière.

Baron

Oh! Don't do that, Miss. Do you want me to quarrel with him?

Armande

He'd be in his rights, for your billet-doux is very impertinent to him. (opening the letter and reading it while leaning nonchalantly on the chimney) "No, you no longer love, you will never love, Molière—right? He doesn't love you anymore. He is much too good for you, you are much too young for him. Trust in a young heart filled with hope and courage. As of yet, I can say nothing, but my love will make you achieve fame and fortune, if you encourage me! Etc. etc." It's very pretty, all that; but Molière will be little flattered by the respect you advise me to bear to his gravity.

Baron

To offend, to denigrate Molière! Oh, such is not my intention. I was trying to prove to myself that this passion he supposedly has for you was just that—a supposition. It was to strengthen my conscience, which was a little frightened, perhaps, that I wrote you in this way. Wait, Armande, decide for me! If it is true that he courts you—send me away! Make me hopeless right away. It only takes a word to do that. I feel that I love you, despite myself, more than I ought. That I love you more than Molière does! And yet, I know I ought to cherish Molière more than myself, and not be jealous, but happy over his joy! Yes, love him, Armande. He is so good! Love him. I will be really happy! (breaks into tears)

Armande (aside, surprised, watching him)

Yeah! There's a good, loving heart. (aloud) Come, come, my dear Baron, a bit of courage, especially in front of people. You let your feelings for me appear too obvious and Molière will end up noticing.

Baron (trembling)

You fear Molière?

Armande

Oh—I don't fear anybody! But, I don't want to get in a fight with him, as you were saying just now.

Baron

He loves you, then?

Armande

I don't know, but since you yourself say so—

Baron

Armande, I don't think—I don't know a thing. I will only believe what you wish to tell me. It's up to you to prevent me from going astray.

Armande (pensively)

You have really got virtue in friendship. It's nice to see in a boy of your age. But, that virtue would be disquieting for anyone tempted to love you.

Baron

What do you mean, Armande? Armande! If you were to love me—

Armande

Well, if I had loved you, and if Molière had cast his regard on me—would Molière's misfortune prevent you from realizing your happiness?

Baron

Why all these ifs? Speak, if you love me and don't bandy words.

Armande

Oh! How the question is changed! First, you asked if Molière loved me.

Baron

How you make me suffer! Speak to me of yourself—of yourself alone.

Armande

No, I prefer to speak of Molière first. Of Molière, who you cherish more than yourself—and you no longer want that?

Baron

Well, speak of him, then, and tell me that you love him.

Armande

Again, that's another matter. You cannot keep two ideas together, Baron. The question was: do I love Molière, and if, in that case, you ought to court me.

Baron (crushed)

Tell me my doom! You love him?

Armande

You are as courageous as a knight! Here you are, ready to be cured of your blazing passion if I say yes. You do not love me!

Baron

Cured! You say I will be cured? Indeed, death cures all ills.

Armande (laughing)

Ah, Baron, if you tell me you will die of it, I will be forced not to let you die for so little, because I am not a tigress—and then—so much the worse for Molière.

Baron

You laugh, you joke at such a time. When I feel I am ready to sacrifice to you my conscience—the first flower of my loyalty, all the religion of my childhood. Armande, have pity on me! I thought that a man's first love ought to be so pure, so sweet—and I would be completely intoxicated by it.

Armande

If intoxicated, you would not be cured. I see that, and you are putting me in mind of a quite chivalrous courage, which works on me in turn. Be faithful to Molière. I will be so, too—and the fear of displeasing our mutual benefactor will prevent me from listening to anybody's love.

Baron

Armande, you are killing me! Yes, yes, smile with disdain—mock—find me ridiculous. Say that lovers always speak of their love. I know nothing of the effects of love. I've not yet experienced a despair like the one you caused me. But, I feel that, to be cured of it, I'd have to give up half my soul. Goodbye! I think this test was a cruel game to rid you of me—and that you sought ways in my weakness to scorn me. But you laughed too soon, and if I am more unhappy than I can say, at least I am not guilty. Don't laugh too much, Armande, I am not a coward. You treat me like a child, but I have some pride, and perhaps I will have enough, this time, to prove to you that I am a man—a man that you want to break and who will perhaps succumb to his sorrow, but not to your caprice. (he leaves impetuously)

Armande (alone)

Yes, he's a man! A strong man, too—and he would have had the pleasure of conquering, despite his scruples of conscience! I laughed too soon? No! One gets in deeper than one intends in this kind of game—and Baron is not the spouse I need. He's young, he's handsome, he pleases with his face and the tone of his voice, but he'll probably never be more than a so-so actor. All right! Now, let's see how Molière's play is prospering at court.

(Taking up her petticoat, Armande gets ready to leave. Condé enters with Madelaine.)

Condé

No, no, I will wait here for him. He'll have to return soon. I am not dressed to be seen. His Majesty is giving me a private audience after the ballet, and while waiting, I want to shake Molière's hand in this retired corner, which is more agreeable to a man fatigued by campaigns and voyages, than the splendor of royal feasts. But, here's your sister, if I am not mistaken!

Armande (recognizing him)

The Prince Condé! Ah, My God!

Condé

Pardon me, if after all the years elapsed without seeing you, I did not recognize you at first. Those years have earned you in grace all they have made me lose.

Armande (simpering)

Oh, Milord. I still have my ring, it never leaves me.

Condé

A thousand thanks (kissing her hand) (aside) Still the same carefully studied innocence. (aloud) You must be an accomplished actress by now. They say so everywhere. (turning to Madelaine) They say so of you both.

Madelaine

We do our best to deserve the honors that the King grants to Molière's company.

Condé (to Madelaine)

Do you know, Miss, that when the news of Molière's glory reached me, in the tumult of the camps, in the doldrums of that life, I was not the least surprised?

Armande

Your Highness remembered that this name belonged to a man you had met for a moment on your travels?

Condé

Miss, those travels have much marked my life. They were too bold, too perilous and crowned with too much success for me to have forgotten the least circumstance. I had made nearly twenty-five leagues alone across hostile territory, with a price on my head. Well, I was recognized by only one man, who through great loyalty and generosity, chose not to betray me, even though he was not one of my partisans and disapproved of my undertaking. That man was Molière, the divine Molière, who, in those days, cut a poor enough figure in the world, but who from his air of frankness, grandeur and wisdom, I knew to be far above the average. Since then, he's never written a play that I haven't read with avidity. I even know The Misanthrope. Corneille was the breviary of kings, Molière, of all men.

Madelaine

Oh, if only Molière could hear Your Highness's words! I will try to remember them, to repeat them to him.

Armande

Truly, I didn't know he was so celebrated. I saw quite well that he entertained the court agreeably enough, and the town, too.

But, I never thought they spoke of him in all the countries Your Highness as been to, nor that his renown was so dear to the Great Condé.

Condé

It's because, living so close to this great star, you cannot see how far his rays extend. And then, it's fit for youth and beauty to be proud of themselves, and not to wish to shine except by their own light. I may add to the list of your perfections, ladies, the praise of your virtues, and as virtue is worthy of glory, I am pleased to render you homage. But I hear a great bustle of noise. Perhaps the comedy is over?

Madelaine

Yes, Milord. Molière is going to rest here for a moment before the ballet. I'll run to tell him.

Condé

No, please, let me go with you. I want to embrace him without preamble and see if he recognizes me at first sight. (inviting her to go ahead of him)

Madelaine

I obey. (they go out)

Armande (alone)

I've really done well to remain wise and to disdain equally bit actors and great lords. Oh, glory! I'm speaking of the Great Condé. Virtue can march side by side with glory. Yes, but they ought to unite to obscure all the rest. Molière, Molière! Jealous, not young, but so much glory—

Baron (rushing in)

Molière's coming! Are you going to put suspicion in his heart and show him my letter? Burn it, forget it, Miss, I beg you.

Armande

Me? Do I have any recollection that you said or wrote something?

Baron

Oh! My God!

Molière (entering with Condé)

I think today is the most beautiful day of my life. The conqueror remembers Molière and wants to clasp him in his arms—for the love of morality and truth. I could never ask of heaven greater recompense than that I've had the approval of the greatest captain and most honest man of his country.

Condé

After Turenne!

Molière

With Turenne! Who knows one, honors the other. And these two great rivals are aggrandized the more by reconciling. Ah, I told you, indeed, Milord, that you would become the Sword of France.

Condé

We'll get back to that—and I really want to speak to you about it, but we have no time to lose here, and I know that your profession needs more order and presence of mind than mine. I leave you by asking you to come to see me at Chantilly as soon as you've finished your engagement at Versailles. (shaking Molière's hand, noticing Brecourt) Ah, sir, before you wanted to cut my throat. Your hand, too, I beg you. Ladies, I am your humble servant. (to Molière, who wishes to escort him) No, sir. Don't leave your post. (pushing him away softly and leaving)

Molière

The great man is right. To our business, kids, to our business! Baron, are you ready? Go, sir. Yes, altogether, angels and goblins.

(Baron leaves.)

Madelaine

I am going to see if the Spanish singers are at their post. (she goes out)

Pierrette (to Molière)

And you, I hope, are going to rest a bit before you start to dance again?

Molière (sitting down)

Yes, I want to. Have I really thought of everything? Ah, I was forgetting the most important thing. The King must go through here to get to the theatre. Perhaps he'll want to use my dressing room to put the last touches on his costume. Run and fix everything, dust, wipe the mirrors, go!

Pierrette

Oh, the deuce. I was already Molière's servant, and that was something. Now, here I am, the King's servant. Who would have told me that? (goes out)

Molière (seated, worn out)

I told you, Armande, that you care nothing about my poor comedy.

Armande

I still know it has been a great success.

Molière

How could you know? You weren't there.

Armande

Don't I know it is good and do you think that I know so little as to question the success of your works?

Molière

I would willingly give that handsome compliment in the wings for a sign of interest while I am on stage. That's where I need a heart to blow a little warmth into mine.

Armande

Didn't you know that I was kept here by the presence of Prince Condé?

Molière

Yes, by the simpering of some palace officer, or by the childishness of Baron, whatever. Nothing pleases you and you are still only fifteen.

Armande

No, my friend, I am twenty-five, and I observe, I reason, I reflect, and I understand.

Molière

Well, as for me, no longer twenty-five, I no longer give my spare time to these cold constructions of wit. It's my heart that leads me in those moments, and I feel that I love, and that I suffer.

Armande (caressing)

And, who do you love, Molière?

Molière (with anger)

Oh! It's not you!

Armande (stung)

I know I have too little merit for that, and that you cherish my sister more than me.

Molière

Yes, certainly. She's worth more than you.

Armande

Then, why don't you marry her? After all, she's eating her heart out to wait on you and has had the time to grow young again.

Molière

What are you telling me? You're a bad gossip. Neither your sister nor I have ever thought of marrying each other.

Armande

As for her, it pleases her to say so. As for you, it's possible you have a horror of marriage.

Molière

Oh, I certainly have, especially since I met you.

Armande

In that case, Molière, by what right do you want me to be so attentive and loving to you?

Molière (astonished)

I don't understand you at all! Don't I look on you as my daughter? Shouldn't you love me as your father? And the friendship I demand from you, perhaps it outrages your propriety?

Armande

Why, yes, it would, if I allowed myself to be carried beyond the bounds of prudence and restraint.

Molière (between emotion and scorn)

You mock, Armande? And you want to play the prude with a man who is too just to respond to your provocations.

Armande (with aplomb)

If you call prudence virtue, Molière, in that case, I have no choice but to leave you forever.

Molière

Leave me? And for what, my God? What whim is this? Ah! She's driving me crazy!

Armande

It's not a whim, and I think I'm being wiser than you, Molière, in telling you, that I consider marriage the end wish of honest souls. I'm determined to get married before it becomes too late to inspire my husband with love; for I really want to be loved, and staying with you, I am not. I'm flattered and courted on one side, and preached sermons to on the other. I love wisdom and, neither the love shown me, nor the remonstrances, do any good, since I resist seduction and don't deserve any blame. So, I intend to get married, I tell you, and you must know it, and my sister, too.

Molière (pale and trembling)

And with whom, if you please, have you decided to marry?

Armande

As for that, I don't know yet. I really haven't thought about it.

Molière (beside himself)

Tell that to the Marines, Armande. You love some one.

Armande

Eh! What's that to you?

Molière (crestfallen)

You're right, it doesn't concern me, and I have no right to question you. It's for your sister to know your feelings. Wait, here she is. Talk together. (hiding his head in his hands)

Madelaine (entering)

What's wrong, Molière? Are you ill? It looks as though you're crying.

(Madelaine goes to Molière, but he waves her away and hides his face again. Madelaine stops, hesitating.)

Armande (aside)

Now's the time to get this over with. (aloud) It's nothing, sis. We were quarreling. I intend to get married and he got carried away about it. I ask you why.

Madelaine (shocked, aside)

Oh, I know well enough. (aloud) But, really, what's bothering him? Speak, Molière!

Molière (rising and making an effort to control himself)

I have nothing to tell you, except that I think this sudden decision is very strange—and the manner in which she just announced it to me—outrageous! I thought myself her friend, her advisor, her protector—and she mystifies me with her decisions! She can keep them to herself or tell everybody. I wash my hands of them. (sitting down again)

Madelaine

Speak up, sis. Why not tell Molière frankly who it is that you love?

Armande

That's impossible for me to do.

Madelaine

But, you will tell me?

Armande

Yes, if you will promise me to keep it secret from the whole world, and from him most of all. (pointing to Molière)

Madelaine

You hear her, my friend. What should I do?

Molière (rising)

Listen to her, advise her of her interests, marry her to whomever she likes—if he's an honest man—and don't consult me further, since that is the whim of her ingratitude. (going into his dressing room)

Madelaine (aside, watching him leave)

My God, how he suffers. (aloud) Look, my dear Armande, I am your best friend and for years I've acted as your mother. Tell me your thoughts.

Armande

My good sister, what I have to tell you is going to upset you. For I am very much to be pitied. I love Molière, and he doesn't love me. He will never love me, and anyway, if he did love me, he doesn't want to marry me. Concern for my honor and my dignity demand that I forget him, and for that I beg you to help me—to get me out of here—away from him, and to pretend that I have a plan to marry someone else.

Madelaine (lost)

You love Molière? You are lying!

Armande (glancing at the dressing room door, which is open, raising her voice)

I am lying? And who do you expect me to love, if not Molière? Isn't he the greatest, the best, the most handsome, the most loveable man that I know? Name me someone I could begin to place beside him! (pretending despair) But he detests me. He detests me, and you condemn me for wanting to hide my feelings from him!

(Molière, revived, rushes from his dressing room and falls at Armande's feet.)

Molière

She loves me! She says so! (to Madelaine) Ah, dear Madelaine, she loves me! I am choking with joy. It seems to me that I am going to die of it.

(Armande counterfeits confusion. Madelaine is crushed.)

Madelaine (aside)

So! The hour has come!

(Madelaine raises Molière and leads him to an armchair where he collapses, annihilated.)

Madelaine

Well, Molière, as you've loved her for so long, be happy.

Molière

I loved her! You knew it? I didn't know it myself.

Armande

My sister is deceiving me. You don't love me.

Molière (rising, transported, and pulling her into his arms)

Armande! My child! My love! My wife!

Armande

Your wife, Molière? You said, your wife?

Molière

Yes, my friend and my companion forever, before God and before men.

Armande (bending her knee before him)

The wife of Molière! Sister, bless me in my happiness and my glory.

Madeleine (raising her and embracing her)

Be worthy of him, my darling Armande.

Pierrette (running in)

Mr. Molière! Mr. Molière. The King—the King is coming.

(The doors at the back open. Louis XIV appears, dressed as an Egyptian, followed by courtiers who wait at the sill.)

King (mask in hand)

Well, Molière, here I am, ready. We still have five minutes. Would you look me over, and see if any adjustments need to be made?

Molière (attentively)

Nothing, Sire.

King

Let's get going then.

Molière

Since Your Majesty has five minutes to spare—I ask one for myself.

King (smiling)

I'll give you two. Speak freely.

Molière

I ask Your Majesty to approve my taking Miss Gresinde—Armande Béjart, as my wife, who will strive to please by continuing her employment in the company honored by your royal benefits.

King

This marriage suits me, since it insures that my theatre has excellent actors. I pay my compliments to you both. (taking a step, stopping and returning to Armande) Madame Molière, you have a great name to uphold! It's not the King of France, but the whole universe, that today signs your letters of nobility.

(The King leaves, followed by all except Madelaine and Pierrette.)

Pierrette (holding Madelaine in her arms)

Well, Madelaine, are you ill? How pale you are.

Madelaine

It's nothing, it's nothing. Have to go dance. LaForet, Ah, my poor LaForet!

(Madelaine falls weeping and crying in the arms of Pierrette.)

CURTAIN

ACT THREE

At Auteuil. A comfortable but simple workroom, lit by a lamp on a stand. A desk with papers spread over it. A closed window, heavily draped, is to Molière's left. The desk is situated between the window and the couch. A door to the right of the actors leads to Molière's bed room.

At rise, Molière is half asleep on the couch, motionless, eyes closed. Confused singing can be heard in the rear of the stage. Then Baron opens the door at the back and comes forward on tip-toe. Through the door this refrain can be distinctly heard:

"The worst evil is to be born,
The only happiness is to die."

Molière (eyes closed, repeats the verse without singing)

"The worst evil is to be born,
The only happiness is to die."

I thought I must be dreaming—to hear ideas like that expressed in a drinking song. That's a strange way of entertaining oneself. (seeing Baron) Ah, you are here, child?

Baron

What? You aren't asleep, my friend? I came to see if you were sleeping.

Molière

And, how to sleep with these fools laughing, gamboling and singing? Even in my retreat at Auteuil—where I, in my room, heard too much. I came to take refuge here, but I still can hear them.

Baron (after closing the door)

But, you're uncomfortable on this couch! You would be better in your bed.

Molière

Beds are made for healthy people. They are trouble for the ill. Mine is choking me, and I almost cannot sleep any more. But, tell me, Baron, what burlesque were they singing just now?

Baron

It's an impromptu by Mr. Chapelle. We've inspired him with black thoughts.

Molière

Is it the first time?

Baron

This melancholy began with Mr. Boileau, who gave a very eloquent speech on some ancient enigma to the effect—the best thing is not to be born—the second best, to promptly die. Mr. Nantouillet agreed. Mr. Chapelle at first argued against it, then came over to their opinion. He has composed some very lugubrious verse—that Mr. Lully has set to a very gay tune—and there they are, laughing, singing, and crying, without knowing why.

Molière

What is man? A being that tries to forget or whines without ever finding the calm of judgment or peace at heart! Always miserable in the midst of gaiety—in despair even while intoxicated. But is La Fontaine still there?

Baron

He left at midnight, finding he'd had enough of it, but without suspecting they had made fun of him and mystified him all the time. He was even more distracted than usual.

Molière

They always make fun of him, but they are fidgeting uselessly, none of them will surpass him. Ah, so, what time is it, Baron?

Baron

I don't really know. It's plain day, and your guests are getting ready to leave. Mr. Boileau has written these verses which he ordered me to give you as a goodbye and thanks.

Molière (taking the verses)

Go accompany them, and then go to bed yourself. I don't like these indulgences and this excess at your age.

Baron

Some one has to do the honors in your place.

Molière

No doubt. And poor LaForet has been up all night, too?

Baron

And, as usual, without complaining.

Molière

My poor children. I have very indiscreet friends, who respect neither your health nor my illness. I'd willingly rent a place for Chapelle where they could go enjoy his company without staying with me. Since you stayed up—they didn't lack anything?

Baron

I did my best.

Molière

And you weren't led to drink, I see.

Baron

Father, I promised you.

Molière

Good, my child. I thank you for it. And my daughter, their noise didn't waken her?

Baron

The baby slept very well and is still sleeping.

Molière

Good, go and accompany them and excuse me again for being unable to do them justice 'cause I'm on a milk diet.

Baron

Try to sleep now.

Molière

I will try, my child.

(Baron kisses Molière's hand and leaves.)

Molière (alone, reading Boileau's poem)

"Your muse
Tells the truth with style.
All profit in your school,
Everything is handsome,
Everything is good,
And your cleverest epigram
Is often a doctoral sermon.
"Let the envious scold,
It's useless for them to complain
Wherever they go,
That you only charm the vulgar,
That your poetry does not please;
If you were less pleasing,
They couldn't complain so much."

(speaking) Thanks, Boileau! You think I have to be comforted for the injuries inflicted by bigots; you think my suffering is caused by their insults and persecutions! Chapelle believes it, too. My friends, you are all mistaken! If I had not other ills to combat, my strength would suffice for the rest. Alas, my most bitter sorrows are not those of poet and actor, but those of a man, and my heart bleeds from so many wounds that I no longer feel those to my vanity.

(Pierrette enters with the little Madelaine Molière, a child of eight who carries a big bouquet of flowers.)

Little Madelaine

It's me, papa. I'm up early 'cause LaForet said today is your birthday, and I have to be present when you wake up, 'cause you like that best.

Molière (taking her on his knees)

Oh, yes, she's absolutely right, your good Pierrette! She knows that my little Madelaine is the one I love best in all the world. (hugging her)

Little Madelaine

LaForet said that my relative, Aunt Béjart, will come to see me today, and she will bring me a big doll. And my little mama, when is she coming?

Pierrette

Tomorrow, perhaps.

Little Madelaine

You always say "tomorrow" like that. Are you crying, father? Your face is all moist.

Molière

No, daughter, not at all! (to Pierrette) Take her. Children don't need to see tears. (to his daughter) Go play in the garden, Miss, and you will return and have lunch with me.

(Pierrette takes the child to the door and watches her go out.)

Pierrette

How beautiful she is! Right, sir?

Molière

Beautiful, like her mother!

Pierrette (aside)

Everything makes him ill, even his daughter. (aloud) Come, sir, now it's time to sleep, since they spent the whole night creating an uproar for you.

Molière

Are they gone?

Pierrette

Yes, and you will again have a peaceful afternoon.

Molière

Sleeping is a fiction for me. Wait, LaForet, I think it's much better for me to breathe the morning air. Open the windows for me. The smell of their wine had risen up to here.

Pierrette

It's true. They perfumed the whole house.

Molière (standing by the window)

A beautiful spring morning. The sun is risen. The birds are singing. There, LaForet, there—the child is running after a butterfly. Oh—that grace—that splendor of life! I've seen her mother almost like that!

Pierrette

Well, well. She's not far off, her mother, and you have only to write to her; she will return.

Molière

She's far away, indeed, far from the path of duty.

Pierrette

Eh! No, sir. She is in Paris, in your apartment, Rue de Richelieu.

Molière

No! I tell you, she isn't there. She's running to the country, the châteaux, the palaces. She has to live the life of a queen.

Pierrette

Bah! She's a little bored here. She is still young, younger than you, and still beautiful as an angel. She loves to preen and to be seen. She'll get over all that, and since she is wise, let her do it. Think of yourself, write your comedies. Don't trouble yourself about other things. Enjoy yourself with your friends. You have some good ones. Mr. Baron, who is like your son, an honest boy, a good actor already, and one who will do you honor. And here—two more of the list who are up early to come to wish you happy birthday.

Molière (still at the window)

Ah, yes, Duparc and Brecourt, my faithful companions. I love them, even though one always make me well and the other always makes me ill.

Pierrette

Bah! He's got a nasty disposition, Duparc, but at bottom, he loves you no less.

(Pierrette goes to open the door at the back. Brecourt, Duparc and Baron enter.)

Brecourt (embracing Molière)

We are bringing you great good news for your birthday. Du Croisy and La Thorillière returned from the King's court last night.

Molière

Ah! Really? Already?

Brecourt

They knocked at our door, telling us. They were broken with fatigue and going to bed, but they ordered us to bring to you permission to play Tartuffe in Paris. And here it is!

Molière (opening the letter)

Finally! Ah! My friends, what trouble this Tartuffe has been in my poor life.

Duparc

I warned you that it would turn ill and that you would be abandoned by the King himself.

Molière

Who would have believed that a King so powerful, so absolute, would have less power in his realm than a band of fanatics enraged with hypocrisy and vengeance? But, we no longer complain, since in the end, justice is done to us, and here is the permission to play signed by the hand of the King.

Duparc

It is indeed true. After years of forgetfulness or cowardice, your great King, Molière, is a Tartuffe himself.

Brecourt

Keep your hair on! Duparc, the King—

Duparc

Damn it all! Let me speak as I please. If there are spies here, all the danger is mine.

Baron

Duparc!

Duparc

I tell you that torture won't make me give over! The King is a man of wit, a gallant man in certain respects. I wish him well, but he has a vicious side. It's that about which he's a hypocrite. A man of voluptuous secrets, and public rectitude, he didn't recognize at first that in Tartuffe, unbeknownst to Molière, there were certain points of resemblance. But, his bad conscience told him. So, much later, and even while swearing to Molière he saw nothing sacrilegious in the play, he let its performance be forbidden for a number of years, exposing Molière to the insults of his enemies and to the slanders of fanatics. If now, he gives in, it's that, by my advice, Molière put energy into his last petition, not enough for my taste, for if I had been in his place, I would have written: "Sire, you are a jolly rogue, you who have three children by La Montespan, and go to your prayers with great pomp—to teach us not to sin." Well, does that make you laugh?

Brecourt

That would have done our business admirably!

Molière

The best thing, really, is to laugh at Duparc's outbursts and the King himself would laugh if he could hear them.

Duparc

By God, no, Molière. He wouldn't laugh at that.

Molière

Listen, my friend. If you respect something in this world, you ought to respect friendship. Yes, I say, the friendship I have in my heart for this man they call Louis XIV. Oh, I know, indeed, my Heraclitus, that you will reproach me for wasting too much of my time, my talent, and my health on him. But I beg you, consider that, if he sometimes ordered me to do hurried works, he provided me the means to develop others that I would never have been able to write, had I remained poor and obscure. His penetrating wit told him at first sight, that, in us, he had something more solid and more true than those brawlers of the Hotel de Bourgogne, who held the scepter of the theatre. Without the decree of his taste, which he already made law in France, we would never have succeeded with brilliance the way we did in true, good comedy, that which reproves the vices of the times and corrects men in their failings. I have a very profound gratitude for the man who helped me to say many useful truths, and whose powerful hand held the whip with which I whipped the shameful actions of the great of the earth. This man, several times, naively opened his heart to me. He asked my advice, and followed it—he gave me advice, and it was good to follow. He avenged me for the impertinence of courtiers by having me eat with him, head to head, before them all, while they had to stand in consternation. I wasn't born an ingrate, and cannot tailor myself to the court life. Well, it is true, I've had subjects to complain of, and that I've seen spots on the sun, but I have no right to point them out to others, and my faithful temperament causes me to pardon wrongs done me, sometimes, by those who oblige me often.

Brecourt

Ah, Molière, it's of you they can say that the man is yet superior to the writer.

Baron (pressing Molière's hand)

Father!

Pierrette (drying her eyes)

All that Molière said of the King, and of himself, always makes me cry, for it's just my story with him.

Molière

Anyway, my friends, that's enough talk. Tomorrow we must play Tartuffe since we've announced it.

Duparc

The magistrates are going to get a kick in the ass, those who still hoped to prohibit it.

Baron

Let's leave for Paris now, for we've only just enough time to get ready.

Molière

Ah! My young friend, you long to see the footlights again. Come on! This is going to help me and make me forget my illness. Help me get everything ready, my friends. You, Pierrette, pack my boxes while I dress. Baron, arrange my papers, I beg you, and shut up all my drawers.

(They all leave except Baron.)

Baron (alone, arranging papers at the desk)

Yes, this trip will do him good, and ill to me, for we will see each other again. She'll have to take up her role in Tartuffe, and whatever Molière says, he's more ready to pardon her, than to cross her. Courage! What does it matter if I suffer, so long as he is happy? My sorrow is a virtuous thing that I offer to heaven for the love of my benefactor, and my consolation is to feel myself his friend, even when he cannot know it. (looking at the papers) Ah, the manuscript of *Les Précieuses ridicules*—is it in order? Yes. The poem by Boileau. Poems, more poems—praise—insults—letters. (taking an open letter) Anonymous letters. And here's one secretly received. "You must know, Elomoire—" Elomoire? Ah yes, it's an anagram of Molière. "The care that his spicy better half takes to change poor Sganarelle's suspicions into a striking, indeed scandalous reality." Oh, this is horrible. "It's the Prince de C, the best friend of the ignoble and diabolic author of Tartuffe, who is now avenging all the deceived husbands whose misfortunes he so cheerfully mocked." (tearing the letter with indignation) And this is what the scoundrels write him every day. Ah! Molière, poor, poor heart—how you pay for the honor of speaking the truth. His wife? No, it's impossible. But, still, ah, that woman is a demon. (putting his elbows on the table, his head in his hands)

Armande (entering quietly)

Hello, Baron. Where is Molière?

Baron (leaping from his chair)

Ah, it's you, Madame.

Armande

Well, does that astound you?

Baron

Yes, surely. We didn't think you had received notice of the presentation of Tartuffe so soon, and we thought to find you still in Paris.

Armande

Still in Paris? Why not say openly, at Chantilly?

Baron

They said—they wrote Molière that you were there at Chantilly, Madame, and he believed it.

Armande

He does well to believe it, since I've come from there.

Baron

What, you confess it?

Armande

I don't confess it, I proclaim it, if you prefer. What can anyone find fault about it?

Baron

You ask that?

Armande (laughing)

I get it! Ah, what a silly idea you've got there. The Prince Condé! Let me laugh. I know, indeed, what they told him, but I didn't think it was taken seriously everywhere, especially here.

Baron

You are gay!

Armande

Yes, truly. I'm in a nice mood.

Baron

She laughs and Molière denies his tears. She laughs—and here he can no longer sleep! She laughs, and he is dying of shame for her.

Armande

Go on! I know very well that if he keeps awake here it is at dinner in the company of bon-vivants who leave the house shaking down the walls. You want to convince me that my husband is consumed by tears when he's getting ready to play Tartuffe and be greeted by applause which will make him quite forget his jealousy.

Baron

You don't believe in pain you do not share. That's the way of cold-hearted ingrates.

Armande (after a pause during which she examines him)

Mr. Baron, you will please tell me where you get the right to reprove me, or insult me?

Baron (troubled)

In my case—in my attachment for Molière.

Armande

If you have no better reason to give me for such outrageous

insolence, I warn you, I know how to punish you for it. Find a better one that will allow me to excuse your ravings.

Baron

What better reason could I give you? Is there a better?

Armande

Baron, there's a worse, but one women are used to hearing without offense.

Baron

What's that?

Armande

Pretend you don't know! As for me, I'll pretend not to understand why you show yourself to be more jealous of me than my husband—and I will take such conduct to be unworthy of an honest man.

Baron

Armande!

Armande

Well, Baron?

Baron

You've a dizzy head, or a completely perverse one.

Armande

Which of the two, in your opinion?

Baron

Both perhaps! What! You want to force me to tell you I love you when you know it's not so?

Armande

Ah, you have such a short memory, Baron.

Baron

I think you ought to have an even shorter one.

Armande

I don't take special note of declarations I receive, but chance made me keep and unearth a certain letter you once wrote me at Versailles.

Baron

You remember, and you won't let me forget. Ah, you believe in nothing, you don't care about anyone, and you have no respect for anything!

Armande

Oh, doubtless. I am very sacrilegious to figure out that men only blame or denounce women they lust for.

Baron

Oh, you have the detestable faculty of besmirching everything your eye sees, and you will make the most upright consciences suspect themselves. But, so as not to confirm you in your suspicions, I shall leave here and never return. Goodbye, Madame.

Armande (dryly)

Pardon me—you will remain, Baron.

Baron

No, certainly not.

Armande (laughing coquettishly)

You will stay, I tell you.

Baron

You think so? You think to keep me here, despite myself, so you can laugh at me, and give yourself the pleasure of degrading, at your leisure, an honest heart, by turning it to peeping and treason to its best friend, and by flattering it with hopes of favors you never intend to bestow?

Armande

There again, the big, hasty word, Baron! If you had hopes, apparently you would remain and find more beautiful words to wrong my virtue, than you have in the service of yours. (Baron, outraged, wants to leave; she retains him) Look, Baron, we are talking madness. Thank God our souls are better than our talk, and we are old friends, that joking ought not to separate. I do justice to your good intentions, understand mine better. I intend to cure Molière of his jealousy; I intend to try to submit to the rigidity of his tastes and habits. I am renouncing all the world's amusements, however innocent they may have been for me. I won't take a single step away from my husband, but how can I succeed in doing that if all those around him push me away or flee to avoid me? I know quite well that Molière's friends hate me. They are jealous of the affection I inspire in him, and their malevolence has embittered my own feelings. Many battles and shames await me here, I know it. How will I be able to stand the boredom of such a shabby retreat if I don't find, at least, the young and laughing companions of my studies?

Baron

No, no, don't talk to me any more. I prefer your hate to your perfidious friendship.

Armande (aside)

That we shall see. (aloud) Well, in that case, let's leave. I will leave in my way, you in yours.

Baron

Do you want to kill Molière?

Armande

And you don't want him to live, since you challenge me to abandon him?

Baron (striking the table)

What is this wrongful and abominable fantasy of wanting to keep me around you?

Armande

And, don't you see your obstinacy in avoiding me is an offense? Why cannot we live under the same roof without being guilty of something? —Someone's coming, get control of yourself and think it over. I hear voices that I know, and which tell me storms are brewing. I will face them down courageously, or I'll give it up—depending on whether you support me or abandon me.

Baron

But, I cannot do anything in these domestic storms. I mustn't say anything—I mustn't even be present.

Armande

Don't leave me, Baron. (with pretended fright) Say nothing, if you like, but don't leave me alone with them.

(Baron, uncertain and apart, lets himself fall into a chair by the desk. Armande goes in front of Duparc and Brecourt to her sister and embraces her.)

Armande

Hello, sis, hello, my good friends. Isn't Molière with you?

Madelaine

Molière isn't up yet.

Armande

Is he sick? I am going—

Duparc (roughly)

Don't go, it's no use. He won't receive you.

Armande (haughtily)

Did he tell you to say this to me?

Duparc

I take it upon myself.

Madelaine

Duparc, I beg you, let us speak!

Duparc

No, no, no more fine manners! I will tell him his fate myself. What! Slut that you are, you have the effrontery to come here in a carriage from Chantilly, leaving the arms of Condé!

Baron (agitated)

Duparc!

Duparc

I am not speaking to you. I am speaking to Madame Molière, and I say to her—

Brecourt

You will say no more, or we will have a little affair. Armande, hear me. I don't know what this trip to Chantilly signifies, but the sight of your carriage entering the courtyard caused Molière to feel ill to such a degree that we were frightened. He pushed us away in a rage, and has locked himself in his room without explaining to us his intentions toward you.

Madelaine

Don't be discouraged, Armande. You know Molière, after thinking things over, always quiets down after these outbursts of sorrow. Let him calm down, and he will listen, I don't doubt, to the good reasons you have to give him to explain your absence and to refute evil talk.

Armande (looking at Baron, who remains motionless)

I have nothing to say against slanders too base to touch me, and that Molière ought, for his honor and mine, long ago, have learned to scorn. As to the reason for the length of my absence, it seems to me that you ought to have been able to grasp it before I did, all of you who are here, and who know what I have had to suffer from the jealousy of my husband.

Brecourt

My dear, I have the right to speak to you as an old friend who has loved you since childhood. Don't be so proud, it's not a disgrace to submit to the hand that loves us. If you are irreproachable, as I'm sure you are, justify yourself, and you will be heard. If you have committed some small fault, love, and you will be pardoned.

Armande

Brecourt, you are a man of sense, and that's why I tell you that if you were in my place, you wouldn't have the patience you advise me to have. My fate is cruel, and I don't deserve it. Molière, has the misfortune of his age.

Duparc

Molière is not so much older than you that you ought to scorn so much his decay. You are already at least thirty, my sweet, and it's no longer the age to play the madcap.

Madelaine (to Armande)

Don't listen to this ruffian, who at bottom you love, and think only of Molière. He is very sick, and very unhappy—trust me!

Armande

I am profoundly saddened by it. But, why do you want me to blame myself? What! Isn't there enough bitterness without adding a shame to it that I do not deserve?

Madelaine

Eh! Who speaks to you of shame, my darling Armande? I know, myself, that your conduct was always pure, and that you live in the world without letting it lead you astray with its seductions. But, it's not in the world, it's in the breast of your family, it's around your child, and Molière, that your virtue ought to find its true luster. You are pursuing a life of dissipation, which is not guilty in itself, but which will become so, because it troubles the peace, the happiness, and the life of a spouse.

Armande

But, why is he alarmed to such a degree?

Brecourt

Ah, my poor Armande, it's because you don't respond to the passion he has for you.

Armande

You expect me to be passionate over him, when I have yet to be passionate over anybody? If that was my disposition, would I have married Molière? Cannot he be happy with a peaceful friendship, which is all I can have for my husband, (looking at Baron and turning away with scorn) or for any man, whoever he may be?

Madelaine

Oh! My God! You cannot love Molière! A heart like his has not warmed yours! You look on him like any husband, a man, like other men! Unhappy woman! If posterity judges you, it will condemn you; although loveable and wise, you could be different. It will say that the wife of Molière didn't love Molière—and that will be in its eyes, a crime as great as if you cheated on him. That's what you have not understood, my poor sister. You, so avid for glory, you thought his name would suffice to make you illustrious, but you failed to see it imposed the duty on you of making him happy.

Armande

Sister, I might accuse you, by saying your assiduous presence and eager attentions to my husband made mine useless and discouraged my good intentions.

Madelaine

I don't understand you at all.

Armande

You understand me well enough, for you are blushing! Look in the depths of your heart, Madelaine Béjart, and you will see if there isn't more than one way to be guilty. Maybe I am guilty of not loving Molière enough, but it may also be that you are guilty of loving him more than his own wife.

Madelaine

Ah, cruel words! Bitter heart! Poisoned tongue! This is too much. Armande! Armande! I lack the strength to reply to you. I see you want to kick me out of here. I will obey, but in the name of reason, carefully replace the friends you make Molière lose. Make him happy, love him. I ask you, on my knees, if you are capable of hearing me?

(Madelaine wants to leave. Duparc holds her in his arms.)

Duparc

This is too much, and I cannot stand it anymore. You must have no shame to try to impute wrongs to one who is worth a thousand times more than you. To your sister, who sacrificed herself to you. Oh, we know it completely, and yet she's never said it, and you, who know it better than anyone—you reproach her! To Molière—Molière whose days have been ruined by your infernal coquetry, like torches which children and fools parade and shake to the winds, to all the winds, to delight their stupid eyes with battles and with their flames! You pretend to be virtuous, do you? You profane the word which does not describe you at all. You don't surrender your heart, you don't have a heart, but you prostitute your cold face to all the impertinent oglings, your banal ear to all the stupid idle rewards, your idle hours to all the promenades and parades where the vanity of coquetry delights. Yes, I say to you, you are a coquette, and the coldest, the most cowardly, and wickedest in the world.

(Armande takes a step to leave. Baron rises and makes a gesture. He encounters the triumphant glance of Armande, who remains unmoved by Duparc's reproaches. Frightened, Baron recoils. Armande loses her color and lets her rage and sorrow appear.)

Armande

I scorn your insults, but since I am exposed to them, in my very own house, without Molière wanting to greet me as his wife and protecting me as he ought—I cede the place to those who want to have it. (in an imperative tone, repulsing Brecourt and Madelaine, who want to restrain her) Stay, stay, you others. For I abandon Molière to you, and forever. Ah, I can really say, like one of his characters: "My house is horrible to me, and I cannot go back to it without finding despair!"

(Armande goes out, hiding her face in her hands. Madelaine falls, swooning, into a chair. Baron falls on the table, head between his hands. Molière enters slowly from his room, in the midst of a silence of consternation.)

Molière

Well, has she gone? (Brecourt nods) Gone, without seeing me, without giving me time to recover the empire of my reason! My friends, don't tell me what she said, what she did. Don't say anything!

Madelaine (to Brecourt who is near by)

He will miss her, you see. Oh, we've got to run after her.

(Madelaine rises. Molière, seeing her, restrains her.)

Molière (making a great effort to control himself)

Well, my friends, let's have enough philosophy and wisdom not to bury ourselves in domestic troubles. We don't have the right, because we don't have the time. We must think of Tartuffe!

(Pierrette enters and leads in his daughter who kisses him.)

CURTAIN

ACT FOUR

At the Theatre of the Palace-Royale, the actors' room. Pierrette and Madelaine (dressed as Dorine in Tartuffe) enter together. Madelaine is adjusting her bonnet with Pierrette's help.

Pierrette

Well, Miss Madelaine, I hope things are going well with our Tartuffe?

Madelaine

Yes, child, the public is charmed, and despite the ill-will of malignant people, Molière will carry it off, I hope.

Pierrette

Oh, the way you play, you devil—they'd think you were a real servant, like me, for goodness sake. Only you speak in verse, and you are more beautiful and more fashionable than me. Do you know you are still pretty?

Madelaine

Ah, Pierrette, I don't care.

Pierrette

That's wrong of you. I noticed that a woman can appear beautiful when she wishes, because I see women courted who don't have two cents worth of looks and—certain others are shunned who are ten times better looking, but who cannot get any attention. My opinion is that I could improve that way, if I wanted to. But I don't have time, that's all.

Madelaine

Come, my good LaForet, let's not chatter—the second act is about to begin.

Pierrette

Oh, wow, let's not let the audience cool off. And Mr. Molière! I hope he's getting nice compliments.

Madelaine

Molière is unhappier than I have ever seen him. He's usually so courageous and philosophic on opening nights—this time he is uneasy and deflated.

Pierrette

Poor, dear man! Perhaps, indeed, he's thinking more of his troubles than his play. And Madame Molière? She must be delighted to see so much applause?

Madelaine

She's sad, too.

Pierrette

Ah, how much courage you must have in this world—and how few things go according to our wishes.

Molière (entering with Condé)

Come on.. The second act is beginning and you enter after the first scene, which is very short.

(Madelaine salutes the Prince and leaves.)

Molière (low to Pierrette who is bringing an armchair for the Prince and performing the honors in a cold and preoccupied air)

Where is my wife?

Pierrette

I don't know, sir.

Molière

Find her, and tell her I am waiting here for her, to go over the scene in the third act. She has nothing to do in the second act, she's not in it.

(Pierrette leaves.)

Molière

Your Highness wishes to speak to me? I am at your disposal.

Condé

Perhaps I'm disturbing you a lot at this time, Molière, but I will say it quickly, and it seems to me that after that, you will perform, and I will applaud, your Tartuffe with a better will. So! Your wife—

Molière (trembling)

My wife?

Condé (roughly enough)

Your wife, yes, I speak to you of her. Your wife spent a few days at Chantilly at the invitation of my daughters, who wanted her to perform with the ladies of their court, a little comic play or something. I wasn't there. I was at the King's camp. I haven't seen Madame Molière at my house, and I don't wish to see her, except in your presence, That's all I wanted to tell you, and for now, I am your humble servant.

Molière

I thank Your Grace for the care he takes to justify my wife. I don't need it. I know my wife is correct in her morals and I have never believed that the Great Condé would want to secretly outrage a man he publicly caresses.

Condé

Molière, you say that in such a tone! I beg you to be sincere, and let me know, if in your heart, you believe what your words seem to deny.

Molière

Does Your Highness imagine that, if I harbored such suspicions, fear would prevent me from expressing them? Oh, how you are mistaken! Just as honor has its rights, passion has its bluntness, and, if I thought the Prince was playing me such a trick, nothing could stop me from reproaching him.

Condé

If that's the case, will you explain to me why you refused to receive your wife on her return from Chantilly because she returned to you in a carriage bearing my daughter's livery? This wretched jealousy is so unlike you, that I would never have believed it if Madame Molière had not told me of it just now.

Molière

Ah, my wife takes Princes of the Blood for judges and confidants over our domestic differences. It's too much honor for her and for me.

Condé

For God's sake, Molière—don't take on this way—or I'll lose patience and I have hot blood. I've never lied in my life, and my pride, as much as my loyalty, will not allow me to suffer slights. How can you expect me to listen through your play with the idea you have of me? I am outraged and would willingly burn down your theatre, rather than stay here. Ask my pardon, by all the devils, ask my pardon, Molière, for I am an honest man, and if you take me for a Tartuffe (smiling in the midst of his rage) I am capable of killing you to prove I am your friend.

Molière (smiling with sadness)

If Your Highness will permit me to tell him the first word that comes to my lips—

Condé

Speak, speak! The first word is always the best.

Molière

Well, I say you are a fine man.

Condé (extending his hand)

Thanks, Molière. I am satisfied.

Molière

Wait, Prince! I am enraged, too, and no less angry than you.

Condé

Ah! Ah!

Molière

I am wounded by the attention the Prince gives to the words of my wife, a child whom I cherish, and that injures me. I am not Sganarelle. I am not Arnolphe. My enemies say so, but my friends ought not to believe it. If I have a kind of jealousy in the depths of my soul, I know how to keep it in, and I don't have the kind they think I do. Mine has nothing uncouth, and does not slander the honor of my wife. All my suffering, all my rage comes from the attitude these handsome courtiers take with me, who follow her steps, and who she is wrong enough to wish to mock, without thinking they intend to mock me. Yes, I hate this court that my profession forces me to live in, where envy reigns together with baseness and hypocrisy. I hate all courts, even yours, Milord. It's a great honor for me to be greeted in your cabinet, but my wife's place is not in your salons. And there, where your daughters, the princesses, reign from the respect they inspire, the wife of Molière, who would also be respected amongst her equals, is confused and scorned by the noble libertines who serve you. What is the dignity and delicacy of Molière's heart to the likes of theirs? Molière, a jester, a comedian—come on—it's too much honor they do him by noticing he has a pretty wife.

Condé

I understand your trouble, Molière, but I find you too bitter against the men of the court, who are not all guilty of their own vices. Permit me to tell you the abasement which their frivolous impertinence masks is the work of a policy you've served perhaps too well. If the nobility has no more respectability, it's the King who has made it so. And you, yourself, have given it it's death blow. He kills with cannons, you killed with satire. And now, instead of restless men, and no doubt dangerous, but manly and strong, you have only effeminates. Libertinism is the refuge of those who have nothing great to do. And you complain of their ills—which are your own work.

Molière

It's because that work is still unfinished that it bears such evil fruit.

Condé

What more do you want to do? Do you hope to sink the nobility lower still? That is indeed presumptuous!

Molière

Prince, do you recall what a libeler of ferocious eloquence wrote about the French? That man was paid by you to torch the throne to the benefit of the nobility, and now from its entrails a cry that you've been unable to contain escapes. "The nobility are great only because we carry them on our shoulders. We have only to shrug, to hurl them to the earth."

Condé

God, sir, you have a fine memory. But whether Dubosq was paid by me, think that the absolute power of one is not a refuge for the weak. You are indeed proud, you and others, because you have permitted everything, admired everything, deified all in a King, who by chance, happens to be a great man. But let this man perish, or merely change a little, be it from age or human weakness, and especially from drunkenness with his power— give him the vices that you blame on us, and you will see if he won't come take your wife right out of your arms. And then to whom will you go for justice when you have neither parliament, nor feudal loyalty, nor freedom of any sort—nothing to balance this authority without law and without curb?

Molière (pensively)

Balance will come from elsewhere, perhaps.

Condé (enraged)

You mean it would come from the people? I reply by saying, if all monarchs are not Louis XIV, all plebeians are not Molière, and we do not intend for a second time to bear the weight of demagoguery. No, by God, no. Bordeaux will never again raise the flag of its steeples and we have forever smashed the seals of rebellion, the amazing effigy of the Republic! You go too far, Molière, and I see where our infatuation with the writers of this century is leading us. We are blind, and the King more so than we possibly, but the blood of the Fronde is not yet frozen in our veins, and we will see if we have to, that the order is not yet quite finished. (leaves)

Molière (alone, pensive)

Ah, the lion wakes! The King must not have given the declaration he wanted. As for me, I offer battle with Tartuffe to the courtiers, and our sorrows are joined. (he remains absorbed)

Armande (dressed as Elmire)

You can say what you like, but my costume is horrifying, and I was not applauded when I appeared on the stage.

Molière (jesting and sad, speaking to himself)

The King! The Fronde, the Future!—And my wife's costume. (to Armande) Very good! You set me on my feet. You are angry with me for having made you change costumes? You want to play a bourgeoise in the clothes of a princess, and a convalescent who leaves her bed with flowers and diamonds like a woman returning from a ball!

Armande

Not realistic, if you like, but the first duty is to please, and no one applauds something that looks disagreeable.

Molière

If you are applauded for your jewels, all honor goes to your jeweler. But, let's stop this childishness. Tell me how this play is going.

Armande

Eh! Truly, I don't know. I'm not concerned about it. Why don't you attend yourself? Why call me here?

Molière

Ah! I—right now I lack the courage for the supreme struggle. This is the decisive affair of my life, Armande, it's not a question of vanity, even less of money. It's a question of life and death for the liberty of my thought and for that of all writers who follow in my tracks. I am engaged in a terrible battle. Take some interest, if you want me to see it through.

Armande

Why do you want me to rehearse this scene with you? I know it completely!

Molière

We've never rehearsed it together, and you are coming to play it all of a sudden.

Armande

I went to study it yesterday at Auteuil and I was not admitted.

Molière

I didn't refuse to see you. I was sick, agitated and depressed. I only asked for some moments to pull myself together and calm myself. We were going to return together to Paris. You left by yourself, exasperated! Instead of going home, you take shelter at your mother's as if you had a horror of the roof that covers me. Finally, until the last minute you left me in doubt whether you would play your role in my drama, knowing it would be ruined without you. You arrive just as the curtain is about to rise, you don't ask me for any explanation of the disagreement of the day before, you get me into a very unpleasant and ill-timed argument with the Prince, and when I beg you to wear a suitable costume, you treat me with extreme scorn. Armande, my fate is hard, and I succumb, and in you I find no support, no consolation.

Armande

All right! Let's rehearse it then, this scene from the comedy which is dearer to your heart than me.

Molière

Which is dearer to my heart! Don't speak to me of my heart, you know nothing of what's going on in it.

Armande

Oh, I know that I am black with rumors there.

Molière

If that were so—if I even suspected you—would I still love you? Do you judge me so weak, so cowardly, as to adore a woman I do not respect?

Armande

Then, you still love me, Molière?

Molière

Oh! She asks that.

Armande

But, if you love me, why don't you let me know; let others see I am beautiful and that I have wit? Why do you criticize my dress, my visits, my conversations?

Molière

You think I'm an egoist because I wish to keep my treasure to myself? Ah, if you loved me, you'd be just such an egoist as I.

Armande

If I loved you in your way, I would prevent you from displaying your genius, from the applause of the crowd?

Molière

As for me, my only distractions from you are my duties. But try, now try, to love me as I love you, and you will see if I don't sacrifice to your sweet intimacy, talent, fortune, fame! Yes, even the love of work, which is the love of ourselves. I will sacrifice all to you, if you want me idle at your feet. I will spend my life, happy to turn my glance from this sad world, and see no one but you in the universe!

Armande

You still love me to such a degree, Molière, after all the pain I've caused you? All my wishes, all my fantasies will still be laws for you?

Molière

Test me, renounce everything that is not me. Love is a hearth fire which absorbs all. A word, a smile, a look of one one loves—are not these the immeasurable wealth that vulgar breath tarnishes and eyes profane?

Armande

Really, Molière, I've never seen you so sweet to me, and I'm touched by it! Wait, I want to please you. Let's rehearse our scene.

Molière

No, no, no more scenes, no more poetry, no more fiction! Tell me that you only want to please yourself with me alone.

Duparc (to Molière, who suppresses a gesture of impatience on seeing him enter)

God bless! Molière, we're doing fine. The public is transported. There are, indeed, some grumblers, and certain hypocrites, who have taken places in the audience to try to cool us off and discourage us. They hope that the delayed appearance of Tartuffe in person will spoil all. But, it's the moment of triumph.

Molière

Is the second act finished?

Duparc

Not yet. Have you rehearsed the scene with Elmire?

Molière

No! I no longer have the strength.

Duparc

What the devil! Are you going to lose your head at the worst time?

Armande

Rehearse! Rehearse, Molière! Success depends on me.

Molière

What does success matter?

Armande

But, as for me, I want to do it.

Molière

You want to? All right! Duparc will prompt us.

Baron (entering)

My friend, we need you.

Molière

Oh, not to have a moment of peace. What is it, Baron?

Baron

Alas, it's Mr. Chapelle, who's drunk as a lord, and who is expressing such great admiration for you in the wings that the play is in danger. Only you can make him listen to reason, and get him to sleep in some corner.

Molière

Cannot you shut him up in your box?

Baron

He takes me for a court clerk, and is calling me Mr. Bailiff.

Molière

Oh, friends.

Duparc

I'll go throw him downstairs.

Molière

No, he's unsupportable, but he is so good, and he loves me so much.

(Molière leaves with Duparc.)

Armande (to Baron, who wishes to leave as well)

You have nothing to say to me, my poor Baron?

Baron

Do you have some order for me, Madame?

Armande

And you, have you no consolation to offer me, after the chagrins of yesterday?

Baron

I pity you, doubtless, Armande, and with all my soul, for not wanting to understand other people's feelings, and to seek out bitter subjects.

Armande

My dear child, I was very tempted to return with Molière, but you abandoned me yesterday, without money or courage, to curses and insults.

Baron

My God, I don't know what support you require. You distrust everybody.

Armande

I want to trust Molière, and you, you alone! I am going to return to my prison in Auteuil and never leave except to play on stage. Will you be satisfied?

Baron

But, it's Molière and you who must be satisfied! What do you care about me?

Armande

Then, you don't want my friendship? You refuse me yours?

Baron

Armande! I am completely devoted to you, you know that quite well, but—

Armande

But what? Why this but?

Baron

I can no longer go to Auteuil. I must remain in Paris to continue the studies that Molière's weak health forced me to interrupt.

Armande

Study of theatre? I'll answer for that. I know as much about it as Molière, and if he is a great author, I am a great actress.

Baron

Oh, surely—admirable! But—

Armande (putting her hand over his mouth)

No more buts! You will follow me everywhere. The world wrongs me. I cannot go without a servant. You are not in love with me, so you have nothing to reproach yourself for. You are not a Marquis, Molière will not get upset. I am not a coquette (Baron smiles), or at least, a reformed coquette. I will allow you to love whoever you like. Is it a deal?

Baron (making a great effort)

No, Madame, it is impossible for me to obey you.

Armande (hurt)

Ah, that's different, Baron!

Madelaine (entering with Brecourt, Molière, Pierrette, and Duparc)

Well, Armande, the second act has just finished to the roar of applause, and it's up to you to carry the third.

Brecourt

Yes, it's your turn to plant the flag in the breach.

Pierrette

Oh, Madame has only to show herself for that!

Duparc

Come, Molière, brighten up.

Molière (near Armande)

All depends on you, Armande. Restore my faith in myself.

Armande

It's not up to me to influence you.

Molière (confused)

What a frigid reply.

Duparc

Come, come, now is not the time to argue with your wife. Armande, bring him back to his business. He is ours, ours, and everyone's, by God! Are you ready?

Armande

I don't know why Duparc says anything to me.

Duparc

Don't go put on the prude!

Molière (forcefully)

Silence, Duparc!

Armande

It's a bit late, Molière, to impose silence on your friend. Apparently, yesterday, you thought he expressed your feelings sufficiently by insulting me, in my own house, and by forcing me to leave.

Madelaine

He was wrong, and he's sorry for it. But now is not the time to engage in a discussion, Armande.

Armande

You're, indeed, in a hurry to reappear before the audience, sis. But, as for me, I'm terrified to be seen in the costume I'm wearing, and not impatient or disposed to expose the marvels of my person to the shame, the scorn, and the despair I'm in.

Molière

What shame? What scorn? Because I've made you take off your diamonds? Put them back on, if you need them, if that's your price, to finish the play.

Armande

No, that's not what concerns me. Just now, Molière, you said lovely things to me, but no one here has apologized to me, and I choke with shame to find myself in the midst of you all, who more or less hate me.

Molière (floored) I hate you!

Madelaine (seizing Armande in her arms)

Armande, sis—what are you saying? What! Don't my tears tell you that I love you?

Brecourt

And, as for me, do I speak to you harshly, and without affection?

Pierrette

And me, don't I serve you with all my heart and all my courage?

Armande (surrounded by all except Baron and Duparc)

There's still someone here who defies me!

Molière

Who?

Armande (watching Baron)

Duparc, and I want to have him at my feet.

Molière (to Duparc)

As for you, if your rebellious humor and bad temper got the better of you outside my presence, you will apologize.

Duparc

Me—apologize?

Molière

You will do to my wife, as I've done to you recently for having blown up at her at the rehearsal?

Duparc

But, God damn—

Molière

Do you wish to outrage me through my wife? Am I your enemy, the object of your singular hate against mankind?

Duparc

Why, by God, you are the only man—

Molière

Look—have done—am I the only man, along with Brecourt that you esteem a little?

Duparc

I swear that—by God! Molière, if you were to think—

Molière

Yes, I will think that you hate me, if you do not do as I demand.

Duparc

Ah, blood of the devil. I will throw myself in the jaws of hell for you.

Brecourt

Throw yourself at Armande's feet—tell her you are a savage, a boor.

Duparc

Thirty tumbrels filled with demons! I can really say this is the first time in my life that I've made an apology to anyone. Have you heard enough, Armande? How long will you make me appear like a fool?

Madelaine

Eh! My good Armande, be satisfied with the words he forces out of himself. Remember your childhood, and don't break with scorn the intimate circle of Molière's old friends.

Armande (after having coldly contemplated Duparc at her feet, she raises him, with a certain grace, and addresses Molière)

Molière, I yield, and ask you only to solemnly renounce your jealousy. I am very offended by it, and no one will ever respect me, if you do not set the example. Confess your wrongs, and I am ready to recognize mine, and to suffer again, if need be, all your injustices.

Molière (with dignity)

No, Armande, you will never suffer any more. I swear it to you. I know there is a fire in my passion, that according to you, is incompatible with conjugal peace. And, trusting to my principles, I will no longer bother you with my jealousy. Think, on your side, I won't say to manage my susceptibility, for I ask no mercy, but to confine your apparent conduct within the limits of your real duties. I know that in speaking to you of restraint and simplicity, I am not putting myself in your good graces. But, before being a lover, I am a husband and father. I have care of your reputation, which you are not protecting enough from the evil tongues. I have charge of the education of my daughter, who needs good examples. I admonish you then, my wife, not from love, but from conscience, to put up with the boredom of a more sedentary life. I have the power to constrain you, but I hate slavery for others as much as for myself, and relinquishing my right, I speak to you, in the name of our common duties.

Baron (low to Armande)

Death is written on his face! Submit!

Armande

Will you help me?

Baron

Oh, with all my heart.

Armande (going to Molière, but looking at Baron from time to time)

That's the way he should have spoken to me from the start. The voice of reason is all powerful to a calm spirit like mine, and I give in, in all humility. Molière, from now on, I consecrate all my cares to you, and I ask you to pardon me for all the harm I've made you suffer. (she kneels)

Molière

Come to my heart! This is not something I claim to satisfy my selfishness. It's for your daughter and your good name, that I confide it to you to protect yourself.

Armande (to Madelaine)

Sis, I've been bitter toward you, and I beg you also to forget it.

(Armande bends her knee to Madelaine, who raises her, and weeping, pulls her into her arms.)

Madelaine (low to Armande)

You are saving Molière's life. Kill me, if you like. You will do a thousand times better.

Armande (to Duparc)

Duparc, you offended me, but I pardon you! I remember the time when you would carry me in your arms for days at a time, saying you couldn't stand children. Do you want to make peace, my old comrade? (she presents her cheek)

Duparc (kissing her face)

Ah, I ought to break it, your nasty head!

Pierrette (who had gone out for a moment)

Molière, they are asking if they must give the three knocks?

(signal for the third act)

Molière

Oh, of course. And good luck to Tartuffe.

(All leave except Brecourt and Baron.)

Brecourt

She's conquered the world. O, fatal power of cold women—will it always govern the passion of generous folk? But, she cannot kill Molière. They cannot, they must not, disparage him, Baron.

Baron (worried)

What are you trying to say, my friend?

Brecourt

I say, my child, that you, too, you are a man of genius. We know it here, we who watch you grow in the beneficent shadow of Molière. A day will come when all will know, if you wish.

Baron (uneasy)

If I wish—

Brecourt

It's up to you to be everything or nothing. You will be everything, if you remember, to be great in any art, you must be great in the acts and emotions of life. You will be nothing, if treason and cowardice overcome your courage. The death of your virtue will be the death of your talent.

Baron

My God! Explain yourself, Brecourt.

Brecourt

You are on the point of ruining yourself, Baron! I saw your eyes and your expression just now. I saw you exchange a word with Armande which quickly changed her attitude and her intentions. That's fine, but, let it go no further. You must live in Paris with me, Baron. Work at a distance for Molière. See Armande only at the theatre. Hardly speak to her, and never even think of following her to Auteuil.

Baron (throwing himself in Brecourt's arms)

Yes, protect me. Save me, my friend! Pity me, but kill me, if I do not obey you.

CURTAIN

ACT FIVE

The stage of Molière at the Palace Royale. They have just finished the performance of The Imaginary Invalid. *A part of the scenery and the props are still on stage. The scene changers are rapidly removing the scenery. The candles spread their light from chandeliers which hang from the roof of the stage. The musicians are packing up their instruments. Some armchairs and chairs at the front of the stage are occupied by spectators, who are leaving or getting ready to leave.*

Brecourt is at the back, coming and going, giving orders. Condé is seated in an armchair. His attitude is thoughtful, while the wits parade around him. The gentlemen and ladies are standing, speaking in loud tones.

A Beautiful Lady

It was superb! It was wonderful. The Imaginary Invalid is Molière's best comedy.

A Fop (offering her his snuff)

No denying it! It's more comical than The Misanthrope and doesn't offend religion in any way. (they go out)

Another Lady (pretentiously)

It's horrible sitting on such chairs. Molière treats very badly that part of the public which honors him the most by appearing at his theatre.

A Marquis

It's to annoy us, apparently. They say he protests against this custom and pretends the gestures of his actors are ruined.

Lady

Then he's ill-bred, this Molière? (A servant comes to tell her that her carriage is ready.) Ah, Marquis, my carriage is waiting for me.

Marquis

Ah, Madame, His Majesty wants this to be manly. (they leave)

An Old Lady (making signs to a wit, who approaches her)

Hey! Sir! Sir! If you please.

Wit

What, Madame? Are you satisfied by the performance?

Old Lady

I would be, except they spoke Latin, and I don't speak Latin.

Wit

But the comedy?

Old Lady

Alas, sir, I didn't hear it. I had eyes only for the Prince, to see if he was giving any heed to my petition. Now, I wouldn't dare to speak to him, for his face looks very severe. Since, you know him, speak to him for me.

Wit

Go, go, Madame. I will speak to him about you. I am one of his best friends.

Old Lady

Shall I wait?

Wit

Not at all, not at all. You'll miss a chair to take you. I will bring you the reply tomorrow, and dine with you.

Old Lady

You will please me. (making a bow to the Condé who does not see her) I am your servant. (she goes)

(Wit remains alone with Condé. He approaches Condé, but Condé pays no attention to him.)

Wit

It appears to me the Prince is unhappy about something?

Condé (brusquely)

Me? Not at all! What do you want from me?

Wit

I thought that your Royal Highness was waiting here for his attendants. Everyone has gone, and I was going to offer to get Your Highness' suite and carriage to hasten.

Condé

That's too over-eager.

Wit

If I have displeased your Royal Highness?

Condé

What brings you here? You want something? I don't give audiences here, but still, who are you, and what do you seek?

Wit

I am a man of letters—poet—musician and painter.

Condé

That's quite a lot. And so? Speak quickly.

Wit

I pride myself particularly on making beautiful poetry and I think my muse, still restrained in the shackles of obscurity, will find applause worthy of its ambition if the Prince, the illustrious protector of letters, would deign—

Condé

Oh, these are verses? Some sonnet?

Wit

It's only a slender sample of my talent, an impromptu on the death of—

Condé

On whose death?

Wit

On a death, seemingly near enough, for what we saw tonight makes one think—(Condé gives signs of impatience and the Wit hurries on)—in a word—It's an epitaph for Molière.

Condé (enraged)

Of Molière! You write the epitaph for a man still alive, who was there before our eyes just now?

Wit

My epitaph was in praise of Molière. But since the subject is not agreeable to Your Royal Highness—

Condé (beside himself)

It's apparent to you, is it? Let's see these verses. I'll wager they are worse than your appearance.

Wit (frightened)

They are not.

Condé (tearing the verse from him and reading)

Molière's in his dark ditch,
They say he's quite dead.

For me, I don't know what to think.

The play's too severe to be by a buffoon— A buffoon! Molière, a buffoon! Go, sir. That buffoon will live for eternity, while you and those like you will be quite dead, as you say. Dull writer of doggerel. Your verse is the type attached to cadavers to fret them. Molière is still standing, and please heaven, he will be in twenty years, to write your epitaph for me, however unworthy of him the subject may be!

(Condé rolls up the verse and hurls it in the Wit's face. The Wit, terrified takes to his heels. During the preceding scene, the activity in the theatre has calmed down, it remains empty of scenery and somber until the end of the play.)

Pierrette (to workers, without seeing Condé)

Come on, is it done?

A Worker

Yes, yes, little old lady LaForet. He can come whenever he likes.

Pierrette

Hey, don't shake this rug. The dust will make him cough.

Worker

You're right. (to others) What do you think?

Another Worker

Is Molière really worn out tonight?

Pierrette

Alas, yes.

Another Worker

Isn't he coming to rest, after the performance as he usually does?

Pierrette

Indeed, he's going to come, after he's dressed. I don't want him to suffer even a breath of air from the outside when he leaves his dressing room.

First Worker

Ah, take good care of him, Miss LaForet.

Condé (who has stood up, to Brecourt)

These men appear to me much attached to Molière.

A Worker

We are at least, sir!

Pierrette

Oh! It's the Prince de Condé.

Worker (doffing his cap)

We are at least, Milord. If you knew—Wait, Miss LaForet, read this yourself. (to the other workers) Listen, everybody!

Condé (to Pierrette)

Speak, Miss LaForet.

Pierrette

Ah, that will be soon said and his good heart will not surprise anyone. He wanted to play tonight, even though he was very sick, and when we wanted to stop him, he said: "Why do you want me to rest at a time when fifty poor workers that I employ—honest men—fathers of families—will lose their wages and miss their bread?"

An Old Worker

My good God. Will you let a man like that die?

Another Worker

Can we stay here until he leaves, to see how he's doing?

Pierrette

Yes, yes. It will please him to see how you love him. But, don't crowd around him.

Worker

We won't go near him. We'll stay by the stairs, without making any noise.

(The workers leave.)

Condé (to Pierrette, who is also leaving)

Don't tell Molière that I, too, am waiting here for him. That would weigh on him, and would tire him even more. (Pierrette leaves) It's nine fifteen. I have all the time to wait for him, before going to play cards with the King. Ah, Mr. Brecourt, I am worried.

Brecourt

Me, too, Milord. Is there another play as biting and as gay as that tonight?

Condé

Yes, surely. The Imaginary Invalid is still a comic masterpiece in which the study of man and the criticism of human weakness is pursued under the facade of a mad gaiety. But, I didn't laugh at it. My heart was crushed with sadness. Ah, to jest so at his own illness, Mr. Brecourt. It's the courage of a stoic or a martyr.

Brecourt (sadly)

It's the courage of an actor.

Condé

The scene where Orgon dies is lugubrious.

Brecourt

And where Molière says, in such a pleasant way, and where the public laughs so much: "But isn't there danger in thus feigning death?"

Condé

And when this feigned death ends the play, it seemed to me he made a great effort in reality to return to life.

Brecourt

Madelaine, who plays Toinette, had to help him, and I saw her blanch, that unfortunate girl, beneath her make-up, and the laugh which contorted her face.

Condé

Brecourt, I saw something worse. Frightful still—and it was noticed by people like me, who were seated on the stage. In the buffoon scene, Molière seemed to suffer strangely, and when he said "Juro" the second time, a bloody froth appeared on his lips.

Brecourt

I know it, and his handkerchief was filled with blood, but from that moment he felt eased, and the things that frightened us seemed a good symptom to him, because after that his pain seemed to ease a little.

Condé

I almost got up and spoiled the performance. Molière restrained me with a forced laugh and commanding gesture—like that of a brave soldier that will not be prevented from dying at his post.

Brecourt (going to Duparc)

Well, Duparc, has Molière changed clothes?

Duparc

I don't know. You see me in a dreadful rage.

Madelaine

And me, in a profound stupefaction.

Condé

What is it? Speak before me, if it is something that concerns Molière.

Duparc

Indeed, yes, Prince, I want to tell you about it, because you will punish such a great infamy. You will speak to the guy and have the son of a bitch put in the Bastille.

Brecourt

Explain quickly, before Molière gets here.

Duparc

Here's what it is. The son of the actor Montfleury, a Mr. Montfleury who calls himself with much emphasis a gentleman—as if he were the only gentleman actor, and as if you, Brecourt, and almost all Molière's troupe, were not as good as he.

Brecourt

Who cares about that? Continue.

Duparc

Well, this Montfleury, urged on, perhaps paid, by the bigots has just presented a petition to the King in which he accuses Molière of marrying his own daughter.

Brecourt

What's that mean? I don't get it.

Madelaine

He pretends to prove that my amity for Molière has not always been pure, and that instead of being my sister, Armande is my daughter—and his.

Brecourt

Now, that's an accusation as ridiculous as it is odious. They pretend to prove it to whom, I beg you? To us, who know this Hervé, the mother of you both? To us, who know you are no more than ten years older than Armande? To us, who have no need to know the honesty of your relations with Molière. Don't the facts, such as they are, render such a slander impossible to maintain?

Madelaine

It's not you they are forced to persuade, it's the King.

Condé

The King will simply glance at Molière's marriage certificate, or quite simply will believe the word of Condé, who saw the certificate prepared and signed it as a witness, your mother being both present and alive. That won't even be necessary. The King won't believe it.

Brecourt

Your Royal Highness will forgive my doubt. The King has not always been surrounded with irreproachable witnesses and he might—

Condé

You are right, Brecourt. I regret not having seen Molière. But the most urgent thing is to run to defend him, and I am going to the Louvre.

(Condé leaves with Brecourt.)

Madelaine

Oh, no. The King knows Molière, and he will not believe him capable of a crime.

Duparc

But, the public will believe it.

Madelaine

It's impossible. It if were only a question of me. They willingly destroy the weak—but him! Ah, don't let him know about it, Duparc. The fuss we make will get back to him. Anyway, a scornful silence is the best reply to rumors that are despicable.

Duparc

As for me, I tell you, we have to create a stir, damn it, and break the skull of this Mr. Montfleury. It's Molière's habit to disdain slander. He isn't revengeful enough. In this way he encourages the insolence of cowards. If this story isn't loudly denounced, many people will believe it! Charitable writers, who lie in wait for the death of Molière, to avenge themselves for not having dared to attack him during his life will repeat the story without quite endorsing it. Others, who pretend to love him, but who are really jealous, will maintain a prudent silence. Your Mr. Despereaux above all! And, the public, which is as ungrateful as a cat, will stupidly whisper it without caring whether it is true or false. That's the way lame, but tenacious, slander attaches to great men and pursues them still, for centuries after their death.

Molière (entering)

What's wrong with you, Duparc—to speak of the dead?

Duparc

Me? I wasn't speaking of that at all.

Madelaine

You feel better, so soon, my friend?

Molière

Much better, dear sister. Why are you both so sad?

Duparc

We are not.

Molière (pointing to LaForet)

And her too?

Pierrette

You know quite well, women upset themselves a bit because they know nothing, and we are imaginary invalids for those we love—right Miss Béjart? But, when you tell us that you are well, you who know much more than all the doctors, since you mimic them so well, we are reassured, and now are as gay as clams, right, Miss Madelaine? (she makes stealthy signs to her)

Madelaine

Certainly, my good LaForet.

Molière

Armande is morose, too. Here there's an air of bad news on some aggravating topic. Let's forget all that, my friends. LaForet, Duparc, go wait for me at home, and prepare everything, so we can dine *en famille* together with Brecourt. Where is he? And Baron?

Duparc

Brecourt was here just now.

Pierrette

And Baron left his costume.

Duparc

But, I advise you to go to bed when you go home. That would be better for you, Molière.

Molière

I'll go to bed if I feel the need. But I will take my milk at your table, and sleep less sadly knowing you are near me. You will chat, you will laugh, and you won't quarrel over anything. Oh, you only have to cross the street, do me this pleasure. It will distract my wife, who is always bored. Must my house be closed at ten in the evening because I am a bad host?

Duparc

We will do as you like. I'll leave you my chair.

Molière

Not at all! Not at all! It will be better for me to walk. It's so close.

Pierrette

Well, sit down, then, and refresh yourself a bit. You never stop—you're pale as powder.

Madelaine

Armande isn't ready yet, Molière. Allow me not to leave you alone here.

Molière (lowering his voice)

Yes, my sister, I want to speak with you.

(Duparc and Pierrette leave.)

Madelaine

Speak, Molière? Wouldn't it be better for you to rest at this time?

Molière

Ah, my dear, there's no time to rest when the hour approaches. When one must settle one's accounts on this earth—and accounts of the heart and conscience are the most pressing.

Madelaine

Then you think you—? (she can't finish)

Molière (taking her hand and smiling)

I don't have any foreboding. Don't trouble yourself. I've seen myself so often but two steps from death that it no longer frightens me. I know that facing this comrade boldly sometimes forces him to recoil or withhold his blow. I hope that once again we shall put it out of our house, but it won't leave. It is very troublesome, and since it must eventually present itself—let's be ready to follow it with good grace when it is God's will.

Madelaine

Have you some instructions to give me?

Molière

Yes, my friend, but first of all, let me ask you a question. In the course of our long and peaceful friendship, have I, intentionally, even caused you any pain?

Madelaine

Why this question? I've never had any cause except to praise your protection.

Molière

My protection. That word condemns me. It's respect I owe you, veneration.

Madelaine

You've treated me as a sister one protects while respecting all the delicacy of her heart and her spirit. As for me, I've always felt the deference that I owe you. I don't know if my instinct appreciated your genius, but it knew the greatness of your soul, and that sufficed for me to follow you and trust you in everything.

Molière

Well, yes. Tell me of this devotion so pure, so beautiful. Have I sometimes abused it?

Madelaine

Never that I know of.

Molière

What? I never made you suffer? I have always been worthy of your confidence? When I swore to you that I never loved your sister and that I would never marry her, didn't I deceive you?

Madelaine

You swore it in good faith.

Molière

Oh, before God, I swore it. And yet, I broke the word I gave you, and that I gave myself.

Madelaine

You were absolved the day I saw more clearly into your heart than you yourself.

Molière

Yes, saintly and sweet girl, you did. But I, did I consult you? Did I wait for your permission to tell you "I love your sister and I will have her"? Haven't I been brutal, egoistic, blind?

Madelaine

Why these fears, Molière? Have I given you reason to suspect yourself or me?

Molière

Ah, no, never. You are such a pure diamond that when one looks into you one sees only one's own faults. Your clarity consumes the spectator. Ah, all the good you've done me, without growing weary of my suffering, you have supported me in the distress of my passion. How you cured me of my vanity when jealousy led me to violence! How you have lifted up my idol when I was tempted to break it!

Madelaine

Where is my merit in that, I beg you? Isn't she my sister, my pupil, confided to my care since her infancy. My spoiled child, too.

Molière

And there are some wretches who have found a way to insinuate an incest into the purest feelings of our hearts?

Madelaine

What do you mean by that, Molière?

Molière

Nothing, nothing! We will speak of that later. For today, I want to commend my daughter to you, your goddaughter, little Madelaine, the joy of my life, the worry of my death. Watch over her, my friend. Make her modest, courageous, and good like you. Don't let her think of pleasing men, let her think of pleasing only one man. Affection, happiness—oh—a good woman! And they want something else! Here's Baron. Be calm, sister, I am resigned to my fate. (to Baron) Come here. (Molière takes both their hands) And now, my children, I feel at peace and submit to everything. I want to bless you, in case some surprise from my illness should take from me—(seeing Baron shiver)—I didn't say my life—but my strength for a while. (to Baron) I have to thank you, you too, for the tender care you surround me with forces you to forget your youth, success, and pleasure! Heaven will reward you, my child. It will give you real power, that is—talent. And then will come glory, and then, hopefully not, intoxication. Do as I, seek out the faults of my works and my acting, while others look at their quality. Never be satisfied with yourself until you arrive at perfection. The day you are satisfied with yourself—others won't be, because they are not looking for it, not working for it. Think of me when I will no longer be there.

Baron (kissing his hand)

My God, how cold your hands are.

(Baron puts Molière's gloves on him.)

Molière

It's nothing, nothing. Let's go. I'll warm up walking. Isn't Armande ready yet?

Madelaine

I'll run tell her you're waiting for her. (goes out by the side)

Molière

I am going to give orders for tomorrow's performance. (goes to the back of the stage)

Baron (alone)

I don't know if I am overly concerned, but it seems to me he's reached his last hour, and his wife is in no way alarmed about it.

Armande (coming from another wing than that which Madelaine went out in order to find her)

Well, are we finally going?

Baron

But, Madame, Molière is waiting for you.

Armande

Couldn't he come to my dressing room?

Baron

Yes, but only to find Mr. de Vise, a man he so justly dislikes?

Armande

He would have found two Marquises and a Parliamentary Councilor.

Baron

He's quite sick tonight, Madame, and perhaps it would be better not to trouble his ears with the names and titles of your brilliant friends. You know he doesn't enjoy dining with people of quality that he didn't invite himself.

Armande

Some men of quality are in no rush to dine with actors. I didn't invite them, knowing, my dear, that you were to be one of us tonight.

Baron (tranquilly)

Oh, you did the right thing.

Armande

I admire the doctoral tone of Mr. Baron who dines in style with Marquises—and, they say, even with some duchesses!

Baron

When Molière is sick, I don't dine. I don't leave him, and don't bring people to his home to annoy him, preferring his contentment to my pleasure, and his society to any other.

Armande

Are you determined to keep me off? Will you always play the pedant with me? Or indeed, is it still jealousy as it was before?

Baron

Before was a long time ago, indeed, and I had so well forgotten it, that I hoped you yourself had forgotten it. I struggled, and I know I conquered. My conscience is easy, as is my heart, and I have nothing more for you than the feeling of profound respect that I owe to the wife of Molière.

Armande

You love some one else!

Baron

And why not, Madame?

Armande

Fine, Mr. Baron. I congratulate you. (aside) Ah, I will be avenged!

Molière (heard at the back of the theatre, speaking to his workers)

Yes, my friends. Tomorrow, Scaramouche and the Italians. Tomorrow, our Imaginary Invalid for the fifth time. I ask you, as a favor, that all be ready so we can start at four o'clock. You know I can no longer supervise.

A Worker

Oh, don't worry, Mr. Molière. But don't go by foot tonight. There's a very cold wind, and it's raining

Baron

It's raining. Ah, I'll run get my chair and bring it here for you. (he goes out)

Molière

What's the matter, Armande? Are you crying?

Armande

I suffer, my friend, a frightful migraine, an incredible malaise and a lot of sadness.

Molière

What—because of Montfleury's petition? Can't you scorn that infamy? Your sister and I are unconcerned by it.

Armande

Lucky for my sister to have courage like that. But such slanders reflect on me and put me in a situation that is odious or ridiculous.

Molière

And you hold it against me that I have such wretched enemies?

Armande

Not at all, my friend. But still, you ought—

Molière

I ought not to be sick, almost dying, doubtless. I ought to have the strength to avenge you. But do you do you think you've given me a health tonic by telling me so suddenly a base slander that my friends have so carefully hidden from me?

Armande

First of all, you see the black side of everything, Molière. I didn't expect you to avenge me in any way, except by resort to the King.

Molière

I will do it. Don't worry.

Armande

As for your illness, you must be distracted not to think, thank God, that I am more ill than you and will leave first.

Molière

You ill? Ah yes, that's your latest fantasy. For some time you've said you were ill and been taking some kind of juleps just like our

Imaginary Invalid we've been performing just now. You're still beautiful and fresh as you were at twenty. You have the roses of eternal spring on your cheeks and you complain of vapors and small discomforts which serve as a pretext to distract you and impose your will on everybody.

Armande

What, my friend, still reproaches, and when I am so cruelly ill?

Molière

Reproaches! If you mean complaints of jealousy, you are mistaken, Armande. Those complaints I have so hidden in my heart that they are dead. I don't rekindle the ashes of my passion. I've conquered in myself this legitimate selfishness of love which, putting all its joys, all its thoughts, all its cares, in the beloved object thinks it has the right to demand the same in return. You, always cold and proud in your freedom, have left me pitilessly in my suffering. I've learned to bear it. Confident of your virtue, I have silenced the weakness of my unreasonable demon, but don't think because of that I withdraw a reprimand that, more than ever, I have the duty to make you hear. Our honor ought to be a concern, and if you have preserved yours, you have not preserved mine. Your complaints and your intimate confidences to two or three hundred persons have rendered my jealousy public as well as your boldness in defying it. Think that the slanders you complain of today with such bitterness—the monstrous suppositions that they insinuate to the public—are not a little your own work and that they would pry with such audacity into my home life without believing it was stormy and troubled? Armande! Armande! Heaven is my witness now that I entered into the bonds of matrimony conscious of my duties in a comic way, but, at bottom was taught a serious lesson when I show on stage suspicious spouses, insulting, ridiculous, and tricked by their fate. I have put into the mouths of the wisest men the precept of confidence one owes to those one loves, and the respect for an honest freedom for your sex. I wanted to put those laws into practice in my private life. How, alas, have you rewarded me for it?

Armande

What are you complaining of, since I was never unfaithful to you, and even you yourself have been obliged to admit it?

Molière (with greater vivacity)

That's not the question. Isn't there a fidelity of the feelings? Isn't there a fidelity of the heart that wisest friendship commands. Were you faithful to me when you ran to parties and meetings with people who laughed at me?

Armande

I was laughing at them more.

Molière

Fine. And when these people come to coquette around you, even in my house; when my house was infected with their odor, when my ears were deluged by their vapid chatter, when they turned my obliging friends against me, you silenced my complaints with a charming smile from your half provoking, half disdainful lips. Terrible puzzle where the word of my fate is not to be found! When these handsome boys, these beribboned snobs, honored me with their humiliating protection, when they forced, despite me, stupid prefaces on my most serious works, crushing me to the ground to free me from some fly that did not annoy me, and which I could wave off with a hand more assured than theirs, when they stole my peace, my serenity, my life. Tell me, Armande, tell me, was your heart faithful, and can I be proud of you and myself?

Armande

There's a lot to be bitter about, Molière, and these men of quality were indeed odious to you! With whom do you want me to live? With your actors, who, save Brecourt and Duparc, have always surrounded you with wrangling, stirring up a thousand embarrassments for you, and sometimes put you in great danger with their cupidity and jealousy?

Molière

I confess my profession has often crushed me. Art makes me live; the profession kills me. I love a quiet life and mine is troubled with a thousand common and wild details. Still, Armande, we are actors, too, let's not forget it, and let's know how to love our comrades despite their faults. It's a hard and difficult profession that demands all for the pleasure of others and they are not given to reserve or sweetness. At the bottom of their hearts, they are good and great, like all men. They are a thousand times more agreeable and affable than your friends at court, and it's very ridiculous, believe me, not to love one's equals.

Armande (stung)

Very well. So, I ought to love Baron, in your opinion?

Molière

Baron? What have you got against him?

Armande

Nothing, since you don't want to hear me, and I'm wrong in advance. I know all your friendship is for him, and thanks to his care, you no longer love me.

Molière

I don't love you any more! Armande, Armande, I reprove you, I scold you, because I love you, always like my daughter!

Armande

Like your daughter!

Molière (troubled)

My daughter! Ah, the infamous public, they manage to soil the sweet love I'm accustomed to give you. They want to poison that too! A feeling so pure, so religious, and which has always been the refuge of my own heart during the storms which have troubled it.

Armande

Don't think of that any more, Molière. I still love the name of daughter that you give me, and that's why I'm jealous to hear Mr. Baron also call you his father.

Molière

Jealous? You jealous of my feeling? And since when?

Armande

Since you honor a person unworthy of those feelings?

Molière

Armande! I beg you, don't trouble my soul for a caprice. You are suspicious, susceptible! How many times have you unjustly accused those around me, not excepting poor LaForet, who would give her life for you and for me! When even Baron would be an ingrate—don't speak to me of it. I am very ill, my poor child. Let me pass my last days in peace.

Armande

Molière, you shut my mouth. I shall suffer in silence. Oh! You've indeed changed towards me, since you are blind to the extent to which this concerns me.

Molière (moved)

What paper have you got hold of there? Let's see, speak!

Armande

No, I see too much danger for me. You will throw a scene, for indeed, you listen to the lies of Mr. Baron.

Molière

Mr. Baron, still Mr. Baron! Say what you mean to say!

Armande

Molière, it's a very delicate matter. Baron has been pressing me with his love since he came of age. I don't care about it, nor does it upset me, but I find this treason to you revolting and can no longer be an accomplice through my silence. I beg you, then, to get rid of him, without telling him the reason. Promise me.

Molière

All this makes me suspicious. I will not give you such a promise until you have given me proof of what you allege.

Armande

That is very easy for me! But, is it a deal? My proof for your word not to breathe anything to Baron?

Molière

I promise you not to mention your proof to him. It's for me to judge.

Armande

Molière has never given his word in vain.

Molière

You know it.

Armande

Read this.

Molière (looking at the letter Armande hands him without opening it)

This letter is rather ragged! Has it been a long time since you received it?

Armande

I received it last night, and it was with an act of indignation that I put it in the condition that it is in.

Molière (reading with a strange tranquility)

"Armande—you don't love, you never loved Molière, right? He doesn't love you at all—it's impossible. He's much too serious for you. You are much too young for him—youth—love—" (reading with his eyes) Yes, a declaration of common fires. (folding the letter) It's a love letter like all the others.

Armande

And you are not more offended than that?

Molière (getting up with affected calm)

I am no longer jealous, Armande. I told you that. But, I'll kick Baron out. His conduct is disloyal.

Baron (at the back of the stage)

My friend, I've finally found my chair men. I had to find them in a cabaret. They are here. Are you ready to go?

Molière

One moment! Let them wait. I have to talk to you, Baron.

Armande (low to Molière)

What, before me?

Molière

No. Take his chair and send it back for me soon. Go, wait for me at home.

Armande

Remember your promise—don't tell him.

Molière

I promised.

Armande

Give me back the letter.

Molière (coldly, but firmly)

Go, go.

(Armande leaves.)

Baron

What instructions do you have for me, father?

Molière

Father! Am I truly a father to you?

Baron

Yes, yes, a tender father, and you will never suspect what I feel for you. My God, how pale you are! Are you feeling worse?

Molière

I feel fine.

Baron

But your hands are not very warm.

Molière

I've got a cold that is killing me. No matter. These hands still have their strength.

Baron (aside)

Yes, they are bruising mine. Is it a convulsion?

Molière

Baron, you ought to know that you have no better friend than Molière! Oh, don't blush. I don't wish to reproach you with anything. What I've done for you came before money in the pocket and happiness in the soul, but also did good for me. But what I am proud of about you, Baron, is having loved you like a father loves his son. And that, you see is not paid back in words. Love alone can pay for love, and if you don't have in your heart true and strong friendship for Molière—Molière is a very unhappy father and Baron has a miserable heart indeed.

Baron

Why do you say this to me, Molière, in such an incensed tone? My God! In what have I displeased you?

Molière

It's that you're an ingrate, Baron, and I have a horror of ingrates, Baron, never having been one myself—and not understanding how it is possible to be one.

Baron

Me—an ingrate? God is my witness, there is no sacrifice I wouldn't make and no torment I wouldn't gladly endure for love of you.

Molière

Protests—oaths! Begone! I scorn you.

Baron

Father, is it possible?

Molière

Begone, I tell you! I am no longer deceived by you!

Baron (aside)

This is fever, this is delirium! (aloud) Molière, let's go home. You are sick.

Molière

I am not sick. I am not distracted. I have all my faculties, all my strength—and I tell you—you are a traitor.

Baron

Molière, I must suffer everything for you. But, if it is true I am guilty—let me know in what way and if it is necessary to atone for my sin, all my blood—

Molière

This is a ridiculous trick, Sir, and your audacity astounds me! It seems to me that at the first word you ought to vanish before my eyes. Know then, that I have no explanation to give you and I won't accept any from you. Leave! I spare you the shame of being publicly driven from my house, but here I am still at home. This theatre is my house, too, it is my sanctuary, it is my triumphal shield and my bed of sorrows. It was here I wanted to raise you to my height, through talent and virtue, so as to leave you, like a legacy, the fruit of so much work, grief, and efforts. You will return here when I am gone, but while I am living, you will never do so, for you soil a precinct that I purified through love of the good and with the language of the truth.

Baron

Molière, I displease you. Apparently I've offended you, and yet I can swear by what I most respect in the world, by your illustrious name, by your glory which is sacred to me, by your goodness which I adore.

Molière

Shut your mouth! Can't you spare me the sorrow of hearing such blasphemies leave your mouth? (seizing him by the shoulders with convulsive strength and forcing him to bend his knees) So young, with eyes so clear, with features so pure—to carry such dreadful perversity in your soul! God! You horrify me and I want to kill you. (Throwing him rudely to the ground)

Baron

Oh—my God! If you were not my benefactor.

Molière (speaking to himself, without looking at Baron)

My God! Not to be able to esteem or cherish one I preferred to all the rest. To have seen the virtue of a king decline—a king I loved with my guts more than my reason! To have been forced to kill in my breast the most generous and greatest love that man had ever felt for a woman. To be reduced to scorn—a man I nourished, raised like my own son! Ah—today is the day I am old, old, old. I'm centuries old.

Condé (at the rear of the stage with Pierrette, Madelaine—all except Armande)

He's still here.

Madelaine

Yes, and we're worried not seeing him return. We came to find out if he's more sick.

Pierrette (coming forward)

Well, Mr. Molière, aren't you coming to supper?

(Molière remains absorbed, standing still.)

Brecourt (to Baron)

You are very upset. What's wrong?

A Worker (going to Condé)

Oh—he's not worse sick; we heard him reciting something with Mr. Baron. His voice has never been so strong.

Condé (aside)

Then he's much better. (aloud) Molière, I've just come from seeing the King. The plots of your enemies miscarry before the esteem he bears you, and for proof, he begs you to come to him to discuss with you the plan for a celebration he wants to give before going to take command of his army. Are you in good enough condition to assist at the King's rising?

Molière

The King? A celebration? Please, would you tell the King that Molière is dying and he no longer has a master here on earth.

Madelaine

Oh heavens! He's really dying.

Pierrette

Help. Oh, my God! Help.

Molière

No, no doctors! No help other than from your hearts. Rest, silence. Pray, pray around me. God is here as everywhere, and the bigots cannot drive him from my soul.

(All, including the stagehands, kneel around him.)

Condé (holding his hand)

He's expiring. But here is a paper in his hand. A last will without doubt, and we must promise him to observe it while he's still breathing. Read it, Mr. Baron.

Baron (after recognizing the letter)

Oh! My God! That's what killed him.

Duparc

What is it?

Baron (giving the letter to Brecourt)

A letter, a mad, puerile letter I wrote to his wife, before his marriage. O Molière, my benefactor, my father. You can no longer hear me, and I cannot explain—and, you are going to die cursing me.

Duparc

Baron, are you guilty of is death? Oh, I'll kill you.

Brecourt

No, Baron is not guilty. He loved Armande, but he overcame himself, and from the day she became Molière's wife, Baron has been worthy of Molière. Dying soul of my friend, great soul of the best of men, if you can still hear me, may anger and sorrow leave you! Depart in peace for a better world, and know that around you at this moment there are only faithful friends.

Duparc

Alas, he cannot hear you.

Molière (reviving)

Yes, yes, I hear him. Baron, come to my heart. Forgive a dying man. Ah—she's the one who kills me. I pardon her. Madelaine, my sister, my friend, brave Condé, my good servants, my workers, worthy men! I am going. I am leaving you. Don't pity me, I've wanted this moment for a long time. But, my God! How a man suffers before being able to die!

Brecourt

He's still breathing! Let's take him home.

Molière (as Duparc lifts him in his arms)

Yes, I want to die at home. I want to bless my daughter.

Duparc (carrying him)

To lose the only soul I have ever loved!

CURTAIN

TRANSLATOR'S NOTE

The epitaph in the text is literal. A rhyming one follows:

Molière is in a dark ditch,
They say they covered him with pitch.
I think he must be dead for true,
Else no clown would be covered with rue.

ABOUT THE AUTHOR

Frank J. Morlock has written and translated many plays since retiring from the legal profession in 1992. His translations have also appeared on Project Gutenberg, the Alexandre Dumas Père web page, Literature in the Age of Napoléon, Infinite Artistries.com, and Munsey's (formerly Blackmask). In 2006 he received an award from the North American Jules Verne Society for his translations of Verne's plays. He lives and works in México.

www.ingramcontent.com/pod-product-compliance
Lightning Source LLC
LaVergne TN
LVHW041621070426
835507LV00008B/371